BERLIN

BRIAN RICHARDS

NEW
HOLLAND

GLOBETROTTER™

First edition published in 2007
by New Holland Publishers (UK) Ltd
London • Cape Town • Sydney • Auckland

10 9 8 7 6 5 4 3 2 1

website: www.newhollandpublishers.com

Garfield House, 86 Edgware Road
London W2 2EA
United Kingdom

80 McKenzie Street
Cape Town 8001
South Africa

14 Aquatic Drive
Frenchs Forest, NSW 2086
Australia

218 Lake Road
Northcote, Auckland
New Zealand

Distributed in the USA by
The Globe Pequot Press, Connecticut

ISBN 978 1 84537 552 2

Publishing Manager: Thea Grobbelaar
DTP Cartographic Manager: Genené Hart
Editor: Alicha van Reenen
Designer: Nicole Bannister
Cartographer: Tanja Spinola
Picture Researcher: Shavonne Govender

Reproduction by Resolution (Cape Town)
Printed and bound by Times Offset (M) Sdn. Bhd.,
Malaysia.

Although every effort has been made to ensure
that this guide is up to date and current at time
of going to print, the Publisher accepts no
responsibility or liability for any loss, injury or
inconvenience incurred by readers or travellers
using this guide.

Photographic Credits:
Brigitte Hiss/berlin-photo.com: pages 23, 28,
33, 61; **Svea Pietschmann/berlin-photo.com:**
pages 43, 77; **Adrian Baker/International
Photobank:** pages 7, 31, 32, 48, 54, 70; **Jon
Arnold/jonarnoldimages.com:** pages 14, 17,
20, 78, 80, 84; **Walter Bibikow/jonarnold
images.com:** page 82; **Robin McKelvie:** pages
21, 35; **Picture Colour Library:** cover, page 27;
Brian Richards: pages 6, 12, 15, 19, 22, 25,
26, 29, 36, 38, 40, 51, 52, 71, 72; **Neil
Setchfield:** pages 41, 45, 49, 83; **Jeroen
Snijders:** title page, pages 10, 11, 13, 16, 18,
24, 30, 34, 37, 46, 62, 63, 74, 79.

Front Cover: *The Brandenburg Gate, symbol
of Berlin.*
Title Page: *Keiser Wilhelm Memorial Church
glimpsed through a large sculpture.*

CONTENTS

MAKE THE MOST OF YOUR GUIDE

Reading these two pages will help you to get the most out of your guide and save you time when using it. Sites discussed in the text are cross-referenced with the cover maps – for example, the reference 'Map D–C3' refers to the Central Berlin Map (Map D), column C, row 3. Use the Map Plan below to quickly locate the map you need.

MAP PLAN

Outside Back Cover   Outside Front Cover

Inside Front Cover   Inside Back Cover

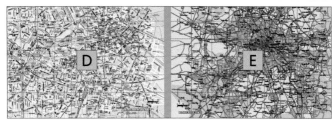

THE BIGGER PICTURE

Key to Map Plan
A – Potsdam
B – Spandau
C – Excursions
D – Central Berlin
E – Around Berlin
F – Berlin Metro Map
G – Prenzlauer Berg

Key to Symbols

⊠ — address

☎ — telephone

✆ — fax

🖥 — website

⌁ — e-mail address

🕘 — opening times

💰 — entry fee

🍴 — restaurants nearby

🚌 — tours

Map Legend

motorway	main road	Hofjägerallee
national road	other road	Gartenufer
main road	mall	ZIETENSTRASSE
minor road	built-up area	
interchange	building of interest	Hebbel-theater
railway	museum	
ferry route	university	
route number	school	
river	parking	P
dam	underground	U
city BERLIN	rapid transit	S
major town ⊙ Kleinmachnow	library	
town ○ Ludwigsfelde	post office	⊠
large village ◎ Glindow	tourist information	i
village ○ Löwenbruch	place of interest	★ Goethe
airport	hotel	(H) HONIGMOND
cave	place of worship	△
castle	shopping centre	(S) Arkaden Mall
border post	police station	●
viewpoint	bus terminus	(B)
forest	hospital	⊕
park & garden Zoologischer Garten		

Keep us Current

Travel information is apt to change, which is why we regularly update our guides. We'd be most grateful to receive feedback from you if you've noted something we should include in our updates. If you have any new information, please share it with us by writing to the Publishing Manager, Globetrotter, at the office nearest to you (addresses on the imprint page of this guide). The most significant contribution to each new edition will be rewarded with a free copy of the updated guide.

Above: *The contrasting styles of the Marienkirche and the TV Tower.*

BERLIN

Berlin, the once divided city at the heart of Europe, now restored as the political capital of a united German nation, never ceases to fascinate and amaze. As the seat of the Hohenzollern dynasty, the hotbed of Nazi terror and the front line of the Cold War, Berlin etched itself into history like no other city. Up until 1989, the Wall cruelly split Berlin right down the middle; just over a decade later, the scars have all but healed and massive building projects near completion. This has been redevelopment on a huge scale, from the grand new **Spreebogen** government quarter to the new embassies around **Brandenburg Gate** and the soaring 'mini-city' of **Potsdamer Platz**.

At the end of the 20th century, Berlin could boast it was Europe's largest building site, but change has not been confined to the major projects. Berlin has witnessed some smaller-scale metamorphoses in its working-class districts of **Kreuzberg** and **Prenzlauer Berg**, while there are long-term plans to transform **Alexanderplatz**, the city's eastern hub, into something more aesthetically pleasing.

West of the centre, the ruined **Kaiser Wilhelm Memorial Church**, as potent a symbol of Berlin as the Brandenburg Gate itself, is a poignant epitaph to the city's destruction during World War II. Its jagged silhouette pierces the skyline at the end of the **Kurfürstendamm** (usually shortened to **Ku'damm**), where Berliners today pour their money into the classy shops and boutiques lining the capital's top shopping street. For Berlin, the future has never been brighter.

The Land

Berlin, spread out in the midst of the flat North European Plain, is Germany's largest and greenest city, with more than a third of its 890km² (344 sq miles) taken up by forests, woodlands, parks, lakes, rivers and canals. There are almost 200km (124 miles) of navigable rivers and canals in Berlin, further indications of the city's waterborne environment.

In the west, the River Havel flows into the Wannsee lakes from Tegeler See in the north; at Spandau in the northwest, the Havel is joined by the River Spree, which meanders across the city from Grosser Müggelsee and the lakes of the southeast. Among the southeastern suburbs are the vast Treptower Park beside the Spree and, further out, the woods and waterways of Köpenick. To the southwest of the centre, near the forest of Grünewald, are Berlin's very own sandy beaches along Wannsee. The green areas extend right into the very heart of Berlin, where the wooded Tiergarten makes a healthy contribution to the clarity of Berlin's air.

Climate

Berlin's situation on the North European Plain endows it with a continental climate of extreme temperatures – it can be bitterly cold in winter and surprisingly warm in the height of summer. The in-between seasons of spring, when the city's 400,000 trees are bursting

Below: *The splendid wooded Tiergarten in the centre of Berlin.*

The Iron Chancellor
Otto Eduard Leopold von Bismarck (1815–98) was the German Empire's architect in chief. He gained good experience in European affairs as Prussian ambassador in **St Petersburg** (1859–62) and subsequently **Paris** before returning to **Berlin** as chief Prussian minister and engineering the defeat of Austria in 1866 and France in the Franco-Prussian War of 1870–71. With Prussia at the head of a united Germany, Bismarck became the 'Iron Chancellor' of **Kaiser Wilhelm I**, presiding over the German Congress of European powers in 1878. He did not enjoy life in Berlin and tried unsuccessfully to move the government to Potsdam. He was dismissed as chancellor by **Kaiser Wilhelm II** in 1890.

Below: *The heraldic Berlin bear appears on the city's crest.*

into bud, and autumn, when the leaves are turning gold, are particularly good times to visit. In the warmest months of July and August, the temperature regularly tops 20°C (68°F) and quite often hits 25°C (77°F). In the coldest months of the year, January and February, the east wind sweeping in from Russia sometimes sends the temperature plummeting to minus 10°C (minus 14°F) or below.

History in Brief

Though Slavic races occupied the site of present-day Berlin from the 6th century, the city has existed for rather less time. Its history can be traced back to the early 12th century, with the founding of **Berlin** and **Cölln** as small **trading posts** at a crossing point on the River Spree.

The earliest recorded documentary reference to Cölln was in 1237 and to Berlin seven years later; Berlin was granted city status in 1251 and Cölln in 1261, the communities merging in 1307 to become Berlin-Cölln (the name was shortened to Berlin in 1709), with a population of some 8000.

The **merger**, aimed at strengthening Brandenburg's stand against the robber barons, was legalized in the courthouse that stood in today's Nikolaiviertel – the spot is identified in front of the **Nikolaikirche** (St Nicholas Church). By then, Berlin had adopted the **bear** as its symbol, probably because of the similarity of the words – the German for bear is *Bär*.

Berlin prospered during the early 14th century and in 1359 joined the **Hanseatic League**, a group of trading cities. Though it clung to its autonomy within the German empire, the city came under the influence of the **Hohenzollern** family, who controlled the March of Brandenburg under **Elector Friedrich I**, and lost its independence.

Historical Calendar

1237: Cölln, a twin settlement opposite Berlin on the River Spree, is mentioned for the first time in documentary records.

1244: Berlin is mentioned for the first time in records.

1618–48: Thirty Years' War destroys Berlin and the population of Berlin/Cölln is reduced to 6000.

1740–86: Under Frederick the Great, Berlin becomes one of the great European cities.

1806: Napoleon occupies Berlin.

1871: Berlin becomes capital of the German Empire. With a booming economy, the population reaches one million.

1914–18: The Great War, after which Kaiser Wilhelm II abdicates, paving the way for a German Republic.

1920–30: The 'Golden Twenties' highlights art, culture and entertainment in the newly constituted Greater Berlin, now with four million inhabitants.

1936: Berlin hosts the Nazi showpiece Olympic Games.

1939–45: World War II leaves Berlin in ruins with approximately 50,000 Berliners dead. The city is divided into occupation zones by the four Allies.

1948: The Soviet blockade of Berlin. An 11-month Allied airlift keeps the city alive.

Above: *The black, red and gold bands of the German flag again stand for the whole country.*

Hitler's Last Days

From mid-January 1945, Hitler confined himself to the **Berlin Chancellory** and the huge underground **bunker** within its grounds – it held a staff of 600. He made his last **radio broadcast** on 30 January. Soon the **Red Army** was within striking distance of the city and by 23 April they were in the suburbs. With time running out, Hitler married his long-time friend **Eva Braun** in the bunker on Sunday 29 April, following her arrival from Munich, where she had been for much of the war. The following afternoon, with the Chancellory under attack, they chewed on their cyanide capsules in a joint act of suicide. The two bodies were then set alight and buried in the Chancellory garden.

Above: *Aerial view of Berlin – the German capital is 46km (29 miles) across.*

1949: Berlin becomes the capital of the new German Democratic Republic.
1961: The Wall is built, dividing the city into East and West Berlin.
1989: Collapse of the Berlin Wall.
1991: Berlin is proclaimed the capital of a reunited Germany.
1994: The last occupying forces formally leave Berlin.
1999: German government departments relocate from Bonn; Berlin is once again Germany's political capital.

Government and Economy

When the Wall came down in 1989, Europe's political leaders were quick to express concern at what effect the rapid turn of events would have on European stability and security. Full **German reunification** was then seen as inevitable but some way off, and the prospect of a much-enlarged Germany, shifting the balance within the European Community, alarmed member states. In the event, the two Germanys became one in less than a year with a combined population of almost 80 million, and the ensuing problems were internal rather than external.

In his capacity as chancellor of the Community's largest member, **Helmut Kohl** was charged with merging two divergent economies. While **East Germany** had been a leading industrial producer of the old Soviet bloc, 40 per cent of its foreign trade had been with the USSR and its economy was way behind that of the successful

Keep Travelling
Of special interest to keen travellers, Berlin's biggest fair, the *Internationale Tourismus Börse* (ITB-Berlin), is continental Europe's largest **travel show**, filling all 30-odd halls of the **Berlin Exhibition Grounds** for a week in early March. There is nothing on this scale elsewhere in Europe to which members of the public are invited. Exhibitors come from pretty well every country in the world – at least, those that welcome tourists – so it is a good venue at which to plan your next holiday.

Federal Republic. Full economic integration was to prove a lasting headache. In addition, East German industry desperately needed substantial investment to bring it up to western standards, and in the 1990s around US$1000 billion was ploughed into rebuilding the former GDR.

The People

No German city is as cosmopolitan as Berlin. Since the arrival of Jewish immigrants from **Vienna** and **French Huguenots** in the late 17th century, Berlin has opened its doors to successive waves of incomers – **Bohemians** in the 18th century, **Jews** in the 19th century, and **Russians**, **Greeks**, **Italians** and **Turks** in the 20th century. The Turks live mostly in the Kreuzberg district, where they comprise nearly a fifth of the population, and also in Wedding and Neukölln; since their arrival in the 1960s, their numbers have grown to 130,000 and they constitute by far the largest immigrant community. Since the fall of the Wall, Berlin has taken in many former **Eastern Bloc** citizens – from **Romania** in particular. In the former East Berlin, the 10,000 or so **Vietnamese** constituted the largest group of immigrant workers. Under Allied occupation from the end of the war until the early 1990s, West Berlin was home to **Anglo-American** forces.

The people of Berlin have always regarded themselves as Berliners first and Germans second; this characteristic was strengthened during the years of geographical **isolation** behind the Wall, when a fortress mentality was all-

Victims of The Wall
At least 125 people died seeking their freedom in the 28 years that the **Wall** divided Berlin. Many reached freedom by sprinting, scrambling or swimming over the border, often under fire. Some tunnelled and some escaped by light aircraft; two winched their way above the wall on a cable stretched between rooftops. The last victim of the Wall was engineer **Winfried Freudenberg**, whose body was found suspended from an oak tree in the district of **Zehlendorf**; on 8 March 1989, he escaped from East Berlin by balloon but, in danger of crossing back into East Germany, had to make a forced landing – a manoeuvre that cost him his life.

Below: *Memorial crosses pay tribute to those who lost their lives in unsuccessful attempts to flee to the West.*

pervasive. It was the Berliners' spirit and self-belief that saw them through years of adversity – the cruelty of the Nazi era, the catastrophe of World War II, the Russian blockade and the divisions of the Cold War.

Religion

While Berlin's present cultural mix makes it something of a religious melting pot, the city has remained **Protestant** first and foremost since the Reformation. Its Protestant population inceased rapidly in the 1800s and now Protestants outnumber **Catholics** in the city by three to one. **Muslims** make up Berlin's next largest religious community; there are almost 200,000 followers of Islam in the city, nearly 10 per cent of the German total, and most of them Turkish immigrants. The city's **Jewish** population was decimated in World War II and now numbers just 10,000 from a prewar total of 150,000.

Language

As in any country the world over, a little effort to speak the native language goes a long way. **German** is distantly related to **English** and is the first language of more

Below: *The Franziskaner Klosterkirche, a haven of peace in the city centre.*

than 100 million people. Teaching of English is now compulsory in German schools, and in Berlin you will generally find yourself understood – but maybe less so in the eastern part of the city, where Russian was taught in preference to English in GDR days.

Music

Whatever your musical preference, Berlin always satisfies. For **classical music** and **opera**, keep an eye on the famous **Berliner Philharmonie**, the Deutsche Staatsoper (National Opera House) and Komische Oper on Unter den Linden, and the Konzerthaus Berlin (Berlin Concert Hall) on Gendarmenmarkt. Works of the great **German composers** feature regularly: Handel, Bach, Beethoven, Schumann, Brahms, Wagner, Mendelssohn and more.

Literature

The period of German Enlightenment opened the book on Berlin's literary heritage late in the 18th century, fuelled by the output of dramatist **Gotthold Ephraim Lessing** (1729–81). Enlightenment evolved into Romanticism and included the works of **Heinrich von Kleist** (1777–1811); in the mid-19th century, Realism took over and the novels of **Theodor Fontane** (1819–98) captured the life of Berlin's high society. Naturalism became the main literary focus at the turn of the century, marked by Nobel Prizewinner **Gerhart Hauptmann's** (1862–1946) effective portrayals of Berlin's working class.

Above: *Germany is famed for its quality brass band music.*

<u>What They Said</u>
Purveyors of the written word have had their say about Berlin over the years:
• The poet **Johann Wolfgang Goethe** (1749–1832): 'There live there bold people, such that one does not get far by being delicate. One must be sharp-tongued and sometimes a little coarse to keep one's head above water.'
• The writer **Georg Forster** (1754–94): 'Berlin is certainly one of the most beautiful cities in Europe.'
• The poet **Friedrich Schiller** (1759–1805): 'That a longer stay in Berlin would enable me to make progress in my artistic work I do not doubt for a moment.'
• Journalist **Kurt Tucholsky** (1890–1935): 'Youth here is never at a loss for words – then Berlin seems forever young, and ever younger.'

Brandenburg Gate
When The Berlin Wall was erected in 1961, the Brandenburg Gate became a key symbol of the division that split the city. When the Wall was demolished in 1989, it became the focus of celebrations as families were reunited. After a two-year restoration, it again stands proudly in the midst of embassies and other important buildings. In the north wing is the Room of Silence (Raum der Stille), in which you can dwell upon the splendid surrounds.
⊕ daily 09:30–18:00
δ free
S-Bahn: Unter den Linden

Below: *The Brandenburg Gate is a former entrance to the city of Berlin.*

☉ See Map D–E3 | ★★★

BRANDENBURG GATE

Previously the western entrance into the city, the Brandenburg Gate is the only survivor of the 18 gateways that once surrounded Berlin, and the symbol of its reunification. Built in 1791 to the plans of Carl Gotthard Langhans, the neo-Classical gateway with its two rows of six Doric columns was styled on the Propylaea entrance to the Acropolis in Athens. The copper **Quadriga statue** – a winged Victory aboard her four-horse chariot – was the work of Johann Gottfried Schadow in 1794; in 1806 it was removed to Paris by the victorious Napoleon following his conquest of the Prussian army at Jena, but returned in 1814 by the Prussian Field Marshal Blücher.

The Brandenburg Gate sits astride the main west-east axis through central Berlin and facing east overlooks **Pariser Platz**, an attractive square that from 1735 was framed by Baroque town palaces. The wide boulevard stretching east from the Brandenburg Gate for 1.5km (0.75 miles) is **Unter den Linden**, laid down as a bridle route from the long demolished **Berliner Schloß** (palace) by the River Spree to the **Tiergarten**, its former hunting grounds. It takes its name from the lime, or linden, trees flanking the wide promenade that runs down the centre of the avenue – generally great to stroll down, but less so into

See Map D–G3   ★★★

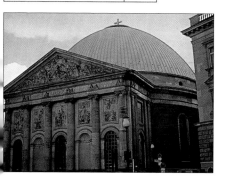

Left: *The design of Berlin's St Hedwig's Cathedral is reminiscent of the Pantheon in Rome.*

the teeth of a biting easterly wind in mid-winter. With the Wall in place, this was the road to nowhere for the people of East Berlin: it ended just short of where the West began.

BEBELPLATZ

Fine buildings take up three sides of Bebelplatz – **Alte Bibliothek** from 1781, the **Staatsoper** (the National Opera House) and **St Hedwig's Cathedral**. But step into the middle of the square to review one of the most poignant episodes in the history of Berlin: here on the former Opernplatz on 10 May 1933, Josef Goebbels' young Nazis demonstrated their warped ideology by burning 20,000 books they claimed were lacking in German spirit. Among the authors whose works were destroyed were Thomas Mann, Kurt Tucholsky and Heinrich Heine, along with the dramatist Bertolt Brecht. A window in the cobbled square looks down on to empty shelves and Heine's prophetic words of 1820 are recalled: 'Where they start by burning books, they'll finish by burning people.'

St Hedwig's Cathedral
🕐 Mon–Sat 10:00–17:00, Sun 11:00–17:00
💰 free
U-Bahn: Hausvogteiplatz

| ☆ *See* Map D–G2 | ★★★ |

MUSEUMS ISLAND

This is the cultural heart of Berlin, and the museums grouped on an island in the River Spree are a rich source of information. The **Altes Museum** (Old Museum), a masterpiece in neo-Classicism, is generally held to be Germany's oldest museum. It was purpose-built by Karl Friedrich Schinkel and reopened in 1966 following postwar restoration. The main exhibition area houses Greek and Roman art and sculptures, while the upper floor houses the Egyptian Museum and Papyrus Collection. The Egyptian exhibits will be moved to the **Neues Museum**, currently being rebuilt, in 2009. In front of the Altes Museum is the **Lustgarten** (Pleasure Gardens), a parade ground for King Friedrich Wilhelm I.

The **Alte Nationalgalerie** building resembles a Corinthian temple atop a raised plinth, reached by a fine twin staircase. It contains 19th-century works by artists such as Edouard Manet, Claude Monet, Auguste Renoir, Paul Cezanne, Max Liebermann, Edgar Degas and Louis Corinth. The dramatic works of Caspar David Friedrich, including his *Abbey Among Oak Trees*, are particularly well worth seeing. The museum's 20th-century works have been transferred to the New National Gallery on Potsdamer Straße.

Largest of all is the **Pergamon Museum**, which took 20 years to build from its foundation in 1910 to the design of Alfred Messel. Highlight of its classical antiquities collection is the three-storey-high Pergamon Altar, which stood at Pergamon in Asia Minor in 165BC. Other rooms contain good collections of Middle East antiquities and Islamic art.

Altes Museum
☎ 2090 5254
🖳 www.smb.museum
🕑 daily 10:00–18:00, Thu 10:00–22:00
👶 8 euro (free Thu 18:00–22:00)
U-Bahn:
Friedrichstrasse

Alte Nationalgalerie
☎ 2090 5801
Other details as above

Pergamon Museum
☎ 2090 5566
Other details as above
👶 a combined one-day ticket for the three museums of Museums Island costs 12 euro

Bode-Museum
Due to reopen in Oct 2006, the museum will have a collection of antique sculpture, Byzantine art and the Coin Cabinet.
👶 free

Neues Museum
Being rebuilt and due to reopen in 2009.

See Map D–G2 | ★★★

BERLINER DOM

Near Museums Island is Berlin's magnificent cathedral, the high church of Prussian Protestantism that was completed in 1905 and was the third place of worship on the site. The first Dominican Church, from 1297, was demolished in 1747 to make way for the cathedral of Georg von Knobelsdorff and Johann Boumann; in 1894, Kaiser Wilhelm II laid the foundation stone for the present neo-Renaissance style building – it was 12 years in the making. The cathedral suffered great wartime damage and its extensive restoration was completed in 1993. Climb the 267 steps to the Dome Gallery – the dome is reminiscent of St Peter's in Rome – and descend to the well-lit crypt, where the sarcophagi of 95 Hohenzollerns are interred.

Berliner Dom
☎ 2026 9136
🖳 www.berliner-dom.de
🕑 Apr–Sep Mon–Sat 09:00–20:00, Sun 12:00–20:00;
Oct–Mar Mon–Sat 09:00–19:00, Sun 12:00–19:00.
🔹 5 euro
S-Bahn/U-Bahn: Alexanderplatz

Opposite: *The Pergamon Museum is the largest among Berlin's rich collection of museums.*
Below: *The mighty Berliner Dom took twelve years to complete.*

☆ *See* Map D–H2   ★★★

TV TOWER

The 365m (1198ft) **Fernsehturm** (TV Tower), built in 1969, boasts the same quality as the reviled Palace of Culture in Warsaw. The most widely held opinion in Berlin is that the best view of the city is the view from the top of the TV Tower, because that is the only place from which you cannot see the structure itself. On a clear day take the fast elevator to the viewing gallery; afterwards, you can enjoy a cold beer or a cup of coffee in the slowly revolving **Telecafé**.

At the base of the tower, quite a lot needs to be done to the windswept concrete surrounds to make the area appealing. The hefty bronze **Marx-Engels statue** by Ludwig Engelhardt that sits in the former Marx Engels Forum is a rather poignant reflection on the 40 years of GDR history. The founders of communism, Karl Marx and Friedrich Engels, gaze upon part of the city that has long turned its back on their tried, tested and failed philosophies.

TV Tower
Each year more than 1.2 million visitors make the trip to the top of the TV Tower, where you can familiarize yourself with Berlin's layout from the observation platform. Have a bite in the revolving restaurant, but be prepared to queue.
☎ 242 3333
🖳 www.berliner
fernsehturm.de
🕒 the viewing gallery is open Mar–Oct daily 09:00–01:00, Nov–Feb daily 10:00–24:00
💰 6.80 euro
S-Bahn/U-Bahn:
Alexanderplatz

Marienkirche
☎ 242 4467
🖳 www.marienkirche-
berlin.de
🕒 Apr–Oct daily 10:00–18:00; Nov–Mar daily 10:00–16:00
💰 free; guided tours in English Sat and Sun at 13:00
S-Bahn/U-Bahn:
Alexanderplatz

Opposite: *The People's Friendship Fountain is a well-known landmark on Alexanderplatz, the wide open eastern city square.*
Right: *The Marx-Engels sculpture recalls 40 years of communism.*

See Map D–H2 ★★★

ALEXANDERPLATZ

When the winter wind blows cold in the western part of Berlin, it fairly whistles across Alexanderplatz, the vast open square that forms a hub of the eastern city centre. It is a bleak and soulless place of concrete, tiles and tarmac, surrounded by austere **GDR architecture** of the 1960s – if ever a place needed pulling to bits and starting again, this is it. In some ways it was better in GDR days, without the gaudy neon signs that now surmount most buildings around the square; there is even a flickering video screen atop one building, pumping out its unwatched commercials over the heads of the scurrying masses.

The square the locals call 'Alex' was renamed from **Ochsenmarkt** (Oxen Market) to mark the visit of the Russian Czar **Alexander I** to Berlin in 1805. It achieved fame with the publication of Alfred Döblin's novel *Berlin Alexanderplatz* in the late 1920s, by which time its fine turn-of-the-century reputation as a prime shopping and nightlife centre had all but faded. Severely bombed in World War II, the square was given its current appearance by uninspired GDR architects in the 1960s; a master plan by Berlin architect **Hans Kollhoff** for the square's redevelopment is still under consideration.

Marienkirche
The attractive little church that, like its surrounds, sits dwarfed by the TV Tower and looks strangely out of place set at an angle to Karl Liebknecht Straße on the vast pedestrian plaza, is the oldest parish church in Berlin. The nave dates from around 1270, though the lantern tower was a much later creation, the work of Carl Gotthard Langhans in 1790. The Baroque canopied **marble pulpit** of 1703 is attributed to Andreas Schlüter, and the large **bronze font** dates from the late 15th century. The 22m (72ft) medieval **frieze** is entitled *Totentanz* (Dance of Death).

Above: *Wacky art is all the rage on Oranienburger Straße, home to the Arthouse Tacheles.*

See Map D–G2 ★★★

ORANIENBURGER STRAßE

Now one of Berlin's most fashionable streets, it links Hackescher Markt with Oranienburger Tor through the middle of the district known as Spandauer Vorstadt (suburb on the way to Spandau). Back in the 1920s the area had something of a Bohemian quality; that spirit has now been recaptured with an influx of bars, ethnic restaurants and centres of culture and art. The bars and restaurants at the northern end of Oranienburger Straße include two old S-Bahn carriages derailed and given a new lease of life.

The wrecked building at Number 54–56 with weird artistic appendages adorning its crumbling and graffiti-scribbled façade is the **Arthouse Tacheles**, which started life as a Jewish-owned department store in 1909 but was already in financial ruin by the onset of World War I. Tacheles was for long under threat of demolition but survived and its flourishing artists' co-operative has turned it into a popular venue with studios, a performing area, cinema and café. To the rear of the building, traffic has literally ground to a halt – a van half-buried in the soil forms one of the Tacheles' odder exhibits. 'Tacheles', a Yiddish word, roughly translates as 'let's do business'.

Arthouse Tacheles
☎ 282 6185
🖥 www.tacheles.de
🕘 daily 14:00–23:00; concerts are staged here from time to time, with performers ranging from fairly mainstream bands to more contemporary groups.
U-Bahn:
Oranienburger Tor

☼ See Map D–E2 | ★★★

REICHSTAG

The landmark Reichstag (parliament) building was remodelled by British architect **Sir Norman Foster** to house the Lower Chamber of the Bundestag, the Federal German parliament. Surmounted by a **glass dome** above the plenary hall, the Reichstag's new parliamentary chamber was occupied by the Bundestag for the first time in spring 1999 after its move from Bonn.

The building has endured a chequered history. Designed by **Paul Wallot** in the style of a palace for the parliament of the German Empire, the Renaissance-style building took shape between 1884 and 1894. The tribute 'Dem Deutschen Volke' ('To the German People') was added to the Corinthian-columned western front in 1916.

From the balcony of the Reichstag on 9 November 1918 the German Republic was proclaimed by **Philipp Scheidemann**. And on the night of 27 February 1933 the building caught fire – widely held to have been the work of the Nazis, giving them a ready excuse to stamp out parliamentary democracy once and for all and further Hitler's rise to power.

Reichstag
☎ 2273 2152
🖳 www.bundestag.de
🕒 daily 08:00–24:00
(last entry 22:00)
🎟 free
S-Bahn: Unter den Linden

New Rail Hub
Berlin has a brand new central railway station in **Lehrter Stadtbahnhof**, close to the new Spreebogen government quarter. It is Europe's most modern and complex mainline station, with four underground levels, eight lines for long-distance and regional trains, and six S-Bahn lines. Construction of the new station started in 1997 and it opened in May 2006; the entire project, one of the most ambitious ever in the city, was completed at a cost of 700 million euro (£480 milliion).

Left: *Sir Norman Foster's glass dome surmounts the Reichstag, seat of the German parliament.*

Philharmonie
☎ 2548 8999
⌨ www.berlin-
philharmoniker.de
⊕ tours in German
daily at 13:00
🗿 free
S-Bahn/U-Bahn:
Potsdamer Platz

**Musikinstrumenten
Museum**
☎ 2548 1178
⌨ www.mim-berlin.de
⊕ Tue, Wed, Fri
09:00–17:00;
Thu 09:00–22:00;
Sat, Sun 10:00–17:00
🗿 4 euro
S-Bahn/U-Bahn:
Potsdamer Platz

Gemäldegalerie
☎ 266 2101
⌨ www.smb.spk-
berlin.de
⊕ Tue–Sun
10:00–18:00;
Thu 10:00–22:00
🗿 8 euro
S-Bahn/U-Bahn:
Potsdamer Platz

*Below: The
gold-coloured
Philharmonie sits at
the heart of the
Kulturforum.*

🕐 *See* Map D–E4	★★★

KULTURFORUM

In the southeastern corner of the Tiergarten, the group of museums and concert venues collectively known as the Kulturforum was largely the work of architect **Hans Scharoun**. Plans for Berlin's new cultural centre took shape in the 1950s and the first building to be completed (in 1963) was the **Philharmonie**, the oddly shaped gold-coloured building rising behind the trees only a short distance away from the grand high-rises of Potsdamer Platz. It is now the home of the world-famous Berlin Philharmonic Orchestra under Sir Simon Rattle.

There is a direct link from the Philharmonie to the **Musikinstrumenten Museum** (Musical Instruments Museum) of 1985, with its excellent collection of string, wind and keyboard instruments from the 16th century – everything can be found here, from ancient harpsichords to modern synthesizers and even a 1929 Wurlitzer cinema organ. On the opposite side of the Philharmonie is the much smaller **Kammermusiksaal** (Chamber Music Hall) from 1987.

Art appreciation comes in rather large doses at the Kulturforum, with no fewer than three important venues. The newest is the **Gemäldegalerie** (New Picture Gallery), which opened in June 1998 and houses a major collection of works from the 13th to the 18th centuries, from Van

See Map E–E3 | ★★★

Eyck to Vermeer, Botticelli to Caravaggio, Rembrandt to Gainsborough. The **Kunstgewerbe-museum** (the Decorative Arts Museum) close by displays arts and crafts from medieval times right up to the present day. The **Kupferstichkabinett** (Copperplate Etchings Gallery) contains an important collection of drawings and prints from the Middle Ages onwards, highlights of which include contributions by Albrecht Dürer, Pieter Breughel the Elder and Rembrandt; also Botticelli's inspired illustrations to Dante's *Divine Comedy*.

SCHLOß CHARLOTTENBURG

Initially intended as a summer retreat for Sophie Charlotte, the wife of the future King Friedrich I, the modest dwelling designed by **Arnold Nering** in 1695 was considerably enlarged over the next 100 years to reflect the growing power of the ruling Hohenzollerns. It is now widely regarded as Berlin's most beautiful palace – a shining example of Baroque architecture that was restored after World War II damage.

Above: Schloß Charlottenburg is a shining example of Baroque architecture.

Kunstgewerbe-museum
☎ 266 2902
🖳 www.smb.spk-berlin.de
🕑 Tue–Fri 10:00–18:00, Sat–Sun 11:00–18:00
💰 8 euro
S-Bahn/U-Bahn: Potsdamer Platz

Kupferstichkabinett
☎ 266 2951
🖳 www.smb.spk-berlin.de
🕑 Tue–Fri 10:00–18:00, Sat–Sun 11:00–18:00
💰 8 euro
S-Bahn/U-Bahn: Potsdamer Platz

Above: *Outstanding works of art on display inside Schloß Charlottenburg.*

Even before Sophie Charlotte died in 1705 at the age of 37, Friedrich I had commissioned Johann Friedrich Eosander to develop the building along the lines of Versailles. At its centre is the **Nering-Eosander Building**, housing the quarters of the Hohenzollerns; also the **Porcelain Room**, stacked to the ceiling with Chinese and Japanese figurines and tableware, and the **Chapel**. The dome was a 1712 addition by Eosander, complete with the goddess Fortuna atop.

The east **Knobelsdorff Wing** is a reconstruction of the architect's 1746 original design, containing ceremonial upstairs rooms such as the pristine **White Hall**, which was formerly the dining room, and the gilded **Golden Gallery**. Adjacent is the **Concert Room**. All feature 18th-century works of French masters such as Watteau, Pesne and Boucher. The ground-level **Romantics Gallery** contains outstanding works by 19th-century Romantics such as Caspar David Friedrich and Carl Blechen, along with several examples of Classical, Biedermeier and Nazarene art.

The west wing, known as the **Langhans Building**, houses the **Museum of Pre- and Early History**, with archaeological finds. The second-floor collection of Trojan antiquities assembled by Heinrich Schliemann (1822–90), the discoverer of Troy, is the museum's highlight.

Schloß Charlottenburg
☎ 320 911
🖳 www.spsg.de
🕐 Tue–Fri 09:00–17:00, Sat–Sun 10:00–17:00
💰 8 euro with guided tour

THE BERLIN WALL

| See Map D–E4 | ★★★ |

THE BERLIN WALL

The sections of Wall that survive on the corner of Leipziger Platz and Stresemannstraße are but fragments of the original 165km (103-mile) barrier that ring-fenced West Berlin, the part of the city under British, American and French control. Its construction followed East Germany's closure of the border with West Berlin on 13 August 1961, on the orders of Soviet leader **Nikita Khrushchev**, to halt emigration to the west. Since the GDR's formation in 1949, three million East Germans had fled to the Federal Republic seeking a better life in the West, half of them through Berlin. While the barbed-wire barricades stemmed the flow of refugees, a few still managed to escape across the border – many died in the attempt, among the first of more than 125 lives lost in courageous attempts to flee to the West.

On 15 August, the building of the Wall (Die Mauer) began – in the eyes of the GDR authorities it was a permanent solution to a problem that was already out of hand, depriving the communist state of more and more of its skilled workers. The Wall, complete with its 'death strip' of **watchtowers** populated by binocular-wielding border guards under shoot-to-kill orders, followed the Soviet sector boundary north-south across the city, bisecting streets and squares, crossing rivers and causing the demolition of anything in its way.

> **East Side Gallery**
> The world's largest open-air art gallery is on a section of the former Berlin Wall, stretching 1.3km (0.8 miles) from Ostbahnhof station to the Oberbaumbrücke. Some 120 artists have painted pictures on the Wall, which also contains the work of graffiti artists.

Below: *The East Side Gallery makes artistic use of a surviving stretch of the Berlin Wall.*

Filmmuseum Berlin
☎ 300 9030
⌨ www.filmmuseum-
berlin.de
⏰ Tue–Sun
10:00–18:00, Thu
10:00–20:00
♿ 6 euro
S-Bahn/U-Bahn:
Potsdamer Platz

Panorama Elevator
⏰ Tue–Sun
11:00–19:30
♿ 3 euro

✿ See Map D–E4	★★★

NEW POTSDAMER PLATZ

Berlin's challenge to become the unofficial capital of Europe took root at New Potsdamer Place on 11 October 1993 with ground-breaking at the start of a **building project** on a scale larger than even London's Docklands. The £1.3 billion development bridging the gap between the former western and eastern city centres was funded by the A+T group, Sony Corporation and Daimler-Benz.

An international team of architects created what has become the huge **Daimler Chrysler** complex, with 19 buildings that took just four years to erect. They include the towering Mercedes-Benz Deutschland building with its atrium sculptures; the triple-tier, glass-roofed **Arkaden** indoor shopping mall with its 110 retail outlets; more than 30 restaurants, cafés and bars; and an **entertainment complex** on Marlene-Dietrich-Platz featuring the Stella musical theatre, 3500-seat Cinemaxx movie complex, Imax theatre and casino. There is also a luxury hotel, the 340-room **Grand Hyatt Berlin**, more than 600 residential apartments and many offices. Fountains and other water attractions provide some relief among the buildings.

Across Neue Potsdamer Straße, the impressive **Sony Center** on Kemperplatz contains the company's European headquarters. Designed by Helmut Jahn, it consists of several glass-fronted buildings clustered around a courtyard

Below: The Sony Center is an impressive part of the Potsdamer Platz development.

See Map D–G4 | ★★

that forever throngs with people. Here is the **Filmmuseum Berlin**, giving a comprehensive insight into the history of movie-making with a strong emphasis on German cinema. Three rooms contain memorabilia of the German film star Marlene Dietrich.

Take Europe's fastest **elevator** to a panorama platform at the top of the entire complex's tallest skyscraper – the views are simply breathtaking.

HAUS AM CHECKPOINT CHARLIE

The chief point of interest in the area of the old checkpoint is the Mauermuseum Haus am Checkpoint Charlie, on the corner of Friedrichstraße and Kochstraße – a privately run, fascinating and usually crowded **museum** that tells the history of the Wall and chronicles the many escape attempts made since its erection in 1961. What started out as a small group of exhibits in a couple of rooms on the street corner now extends above several shop fronts along Friedrichstraße and contains photos, graphic accounts of escape attempts and some of the equipment used by refugees – from a hot-air balloon to skilfully adapted vehicles and specially constructed suitcases.

Permanent **exhibitions** include 'Berlin: From a Front Line City to a Bridge in Europe' and 'Painters Interpret the Wall'. Another exhibition, 'From Gandhi to Walesa', takes a wider view of the non-violent struggle for human rights. There are also showings of **documentary films** on the division of Germany.

Above: The Haus am Checkpoint Charlie tells the story of the Berlin Wall.

Haus am Checkpoint Charlie
☎ 253 7250
🖳 www.mauer
museum.de
🕘 daily 09:00–22:00
💰 9.50 euro
U-Bahn: Kochstraße

See Map D–I5 | ★★

Above: *Turkish snacks for sale in Kreuzberg district.*

KREUZBERG

For an authentic taste of the Orient, take the U-Bahn to Kottbusser Tor, sidestep the rather good fruit and vegetable market, get a whiff of spicy eastern food cooking, and head down Adalbertstraße towards **Oranienstraße**, the main drag that splices Kreuzberg's eastern quarter. At its colourful heart, Kreuzberg resembles an Oriental bazaar where you can buy just about anything.

An insight into the fascinating history of the district is recalled in the **Kreuzberg Museum**, housed in a disused factory at Adalbertstraße 95, among the unattractive apartment blocks around Kottbusser Tor U-Bahn station. A short way south of Kottbusser Tor, on Maybachufer – the south bank of the Landwehrkanal – the atmospheric open-air **Turkish Market** takes place on Tuesday and Friday afternoons. There is no better place for experiencing the sights, sounds and smells of the Orient this side of Istanbul.

Kreuzberg Museum
☎ 5058 5233
🖥 www.kreuzberg
museum.de
🕐 Wed–Sun
12:00–18:00
💰 free
U-Bahn: Kottbusser
Tor

See Map G	★★

Jüdischer Friedhof
(Jewish Cemetery)
✉ Schönhauser Allee
🕒 Mon–Thu 08:00–
16:00, Fri 08:00–13:00
Male visitors are
requested to keep
their heads covered.
💰 free
U-Bahn:
Senefelderplatz

PRENZLAUER BERG

Like Kreuzberg, the inner suburb northeast
of the centre that the locals call Prenzl'berg
was jammed up against the Wall, its crowded
tenement buildings suffering from neglect
and the whole area distinctly run-down.
Similarly, since the Wall was removed, much
of this one-time working-class district has
been given a facelift. It now houses a large
student population and is among Berlin's
more fashionable eating and drinking areas,
sporting cafés, restaurants and the delightful
watering holes the Germans call Kneipen.

In the **Jewish Cemetery**, in use since 1827,
rest painter Max Liebermann (1847–1935),
publisher Leopold Ullstein (1826–99) and
composer Giacomo Meyerbeer (1791–1864).

The hub of the revived district is
Kollwitzplatz, named after the Berlin artist
Käthe Kollwitz, whose statue sits in the
middle of the park. Her sympathetic portrayals of the working-class people of
Prenzlauer Berg among whom she lived and
worked for 50 years earned her a place in
their hearts. Many of her works are dis-
played in the Käthe Kollwitz Museum on
Fasanenstraße in Charlottenburg.

Left: *Kollwitzplatz,
with its restored
buildings and
expanding restaurant
and nightlife scene,
is at the heart of
Prenzlauer Berg.*

See Map E–F3   ★★

LICHTENBERG

The suburb of Lichtenberg lies beyond Friedrichshain, to the southeast of the city centre. Here is Berlin's second zoo, the **Tierpark Friedrichsfelde**, covering some 160ha (395 acres) and boasting a collection of 8000 animals of almost 1000 species drawn from five continents. The Tierpark ranks among the largest zoos in Europe. It occupies grounds that once belonged to the Baroque **Schloß Friedrichsfelde** (Friedrichsfelde Palace), which was completed in 1695; nowadays concerts are often staged there.

About 2km (1 mile) southeast of the zoo, in the adjacent suburb of Karlshorst, is the **Deutsch-Russisches-Museum Berlin-Karlshorst**. This was the place where the German Wehrmacht signed its unconditional surrender on the night of 8 May 1945, officially bringing World War II to an end in Europe. The museum reopened in 1995 and contains an exhibit highlighting German-Soviet relations from 1917 until reunification. It is situated at Zwieseler Straße 4, at the junction with Rheinsteinstraße, about 1km (0.5 mile) from Karlshorst S-Bahn.

Tierpark Friedrichsfelde
☎ 515 310
🖳 www.tierpark-berlin.de
🕐 Mar–Sep daily 09:00–19:00; other times of year 09:00–16:00/18:00
💰 10 euro
U-Bahn: Tierpark

Museum Berlin-Karlshorst
🖳 www.museum-karlshorst.de
🕐 Tue–Sun 10:00–18:00
💰 free
S-Bahn: Karlshorst

Below: *Concerts are frequently staged at Schloß Friedrichsfelde.*

See Map D–C6 | ★★

SCHÖNEBERG

The name of this southern district means 'beautiful mountain' – in reality a small rise atop which sits the imposing **Rathaus Schöneberg** (Schöneberg Town Hall) on Martin-Luther-Straße. From its steps, US President John F Kennedy made his famous speech to the people of Berlin in June 1963; after Kennedy's

Above: *US President John F Kennedy famously spoke from the steps of the Rathaus Schöneberg.*

murder on 22 November that year the square in front was renamed in his honour. The building was completed in 1914; in its 70m (230ft) tower is the **Liberty Bell**, a replica of the famous Philadelphia original, that was presented by the US Government in 1950. The Rathaus Schöneberg served as West Berlin's Town Hall up to 1990, when the city's administration became centralized in the Red Town Hall.

Located about 2km (1 mile) northeast of the Rathaus is the Kleistpark, a former botanical garden taking the name of the Romantic poet, Heinrich von Kleist. At the entrance to the park along Potsdamer Straße are the **Königskolonnaden** (Royal Colonnades) of 1780, the work of Karl von Gontard, who designed the domes of the French and German Cathedrals on Gendarmenmarkt. They were moved to their present site from Alexanderplatz in 1910, when the **Kammergericht** (Supreme Court of Justice) was being built within the

Rathaus Schöneberg
☎ 75600
🕓 daily 10:00–17:00
(for Liberty Bell)
U-Bahn: Rathaus Schöneberg

Right: *The replica Liberty Bell in Rathaus Schöneberg.*

See Map D–C5   ★

Sweet Talk
With the Wall in place, visiting US president **John F Kennedy** made his famous Cold War speech from the steps of the **Rathaus Schöneberg** in June 1963. His speech concluded with the immortal words: 'All free men, wherever they may live, are citizens of Berlin, and therefore, as a free man, I take pride in the words *"Ich bin ein Berliner"*.' What Kennedy's scriptwriters had not appreciated was that to Berlin's citizens, 'Berliner' is a popular shortened version of *Berliner Pfannkuchen*. Their leader had therefore informed his host city: 'I am a doughnut.'

The Gay City
Today more than 100 **gay bars** flourish in Berlin, many of them around Nollendorf-platz. Berlin's large gay population suffered persecution under the Nazis and a considerable number were dispatched to concentration camps – a triangular **plaque** in the wall outside Nollendorfplatz U-Bahn station recalls their plight.

---

park. This was later to become the Nazi People's Court, where political opponents received their show trial and were sent for execution, usually in Plötzensee prison. After the war the building stood empty for much of the time, but since 1990 it has again been used by the Supreme Court.

Just to the north of here is **Winterfeldplatz**, the setting for an excellent twice-weekly market and the towering **St Matthias-Kirche**.

Nearby **Nollendorfplatz**, another two blocks north, was a hub of Berlin nightlife and the centre of the city's gay community in the 1920s and 1930s – a period from which the **Metropol**, built in 1906, survives. The latter now hosts events for the gay community and is a popular venue for fans of pop, rock, Indie and punk music. At Nollendorfstraße 17 lived British author Christopher Isherwood, whose tales of the city in *Goodbye to Berlin* were the inspiration behind the film *Cabaret*.

See Map B   ★

SPANDAU

Spandau is older than Berlin itself and was only incorporated into the city in 1920. The mostly pedestrianized **Altstadt** (Old Town), a few minutes' walk west of the Zitadelle, contains some interesting buildings, oldest among them the 15th-century **Gotisches Haus** (Gothic House) at Breite Straße 32 – first turning on your left across the Havel bridge. During restoration work, foundations of a 13th-century town house were discovered in its basement – it is Berlin's oldest residential building.

On Reformationsplatz is the elegant 15th-century **Nikolaikirche**. Its treasures include a bronze baptismal font from 1398, a late-Renaissance altar from 1582 and a Baroque pulpit of 1714. The statue before the red-brick tower is of the Brandenburg leader Elector Joachim II, whose conversion to Lutheranism in 1539 was responsible for sparking the Reformation that spread throughout the March of Brandenburg. From a corner of the square next to the Nikolaikirche, Mönchstraße leads to the **Marktplatz**, with its lively and interesting market.

Gotisches Haus
☎ 333 9388
🕐 Mon–Fri 10:00–17:00, Sat 10:00–13:00
🎟 free
U-Bahn: Altstadt Spandau

Nicolaikirche
☎ 333 5639
🕐 Wed 10:00–16:00, Thu 10:00–17:00, Fri 14:00–18:00, Sat 11:00–15:00, Sun 14:00–16:00
🎟 free
U-Bahn: Altstadt Spandau

Below: *The red-brick Nikolaikirche contains many treasures.*

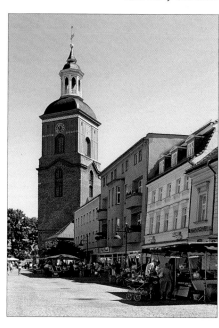

See Map A–B4 ★

Schloß Sanssouci
☎ 0331 969 4202
🕐 Tue–Sun
09:00–17:00 in
Apr–Oct, 09:00–
16:00 in Nov–Mar.
💰 8 euro (palace and
exhibitions)
S-Bahn: Potsdam
Hauptbahnhof

Filmpark Babelsberg
☎ 0331 721 2717
🖥 www.filmpark.de
🕐 Mar–Oct, daily
10:00–18:00 (allow
four hours)
💰 17 euro
S-Bahn: Babelsberg

SCHLOß SANSSOUCI

The Sanssouci Palace is Potsdam's showpiece, designed in 1747 by architect **Georg von Knobelsdorff** as a summer country retreat for Friedrich II (**Frederick the Great**). 'Sanssouci' translates into the 18th-century equivalent of 'no worries' and there could be no better name for a building that provided such perfect relaxation away from the cares of state.

The single-storey Rococo palace is surmounted by a green dome; behind it, wide steps lead down through a steeply terraced vineyard and past an array of sculptures to the **Great Fountain** and small **lake**. Among the collection of opulent rooms within the palace are the stunning **Konzertsaal** (Concert Hall), the impressive **Marmorsaal** (Marble Hall) and the **Voltaire Zimmer**, named after the French philosopher, a frequent guest, and decorated with colourful birds. The palace suffered a fair amount of neglect under the GDR administration, but since 1990 has regained its former glory with a place among UNESCO's World Heritage Sites.

Right: *The attractive Chinese Tea House at Schloß Sanssouci.*

See Maps E–C5 & C–B2 ★

FILMPARK BABELSBERG

Filmpark Babelsberg, located on Grossbeerenstraße, has an important place in German film history – the huge 450,000m² (538,200 sq yd) site, the studios of the former GDR film company DEFA, is among the oldest and largest of its kind in the world. Among the films shot here were *Metropolis*, by Fritz Lang; *The Blue Angel*, starring a young Marlene Dietrich; and *The Never Ending Story*.

The studios are now marketed as a 'movie adventure park', with guided behind-the-scenes tours, special effects exhibits and a spectacular stunt show.

Above: *Sachsenhausen is a memorial to more than 100,000 prisoners who died.*

SACHSENHAUSEN

The Sachsenhausen **concentration camp** set up in 1936 by the Nazis on the site of a former brewery near Oranienburg, some 35km (22 miles) northwest of Berlin, has since 1961 been a memorial to more than 100,000 prisoners who died within its walls. Two **museums** recall the horrors of life in the 'Lager', complete with film footage (definitely unsuitable for children). Two **barrack huts** have been reconstructed on the site, which also contains the **crematorium** and **Station Z extermination site**, where prisoners were executed by a shot in the back of the neck. From August 1945 until March 1950, Sachsenhausen served as a Soviet internment and disciplinary camp.

Sachsenhausen
☎ 0330 120 00
💻 www.gedenkstaette-sachsenhausen.de
🕐 Tue–Sun 08:30–18:00 Apr–Sep, 08:30–16:30 Oct–Mar
💰 free
S-Bahn: Oranienburg

Below: *The gaily decorated façade of the Tränenpalast theatre on Friedrichstraße.*

Architecture
Friedrichstraße U-Bahn and S-Bahn Station

Past the Internationales Handelszentrum trade centre is this station. Before 1990, it was the principal border-crossing point for travellers to East Berlin; for East Berliners it was the end of the line. Outside the station is the **Tränenpalast** (Palace of Tears), now a theatre but once the building through which Western visitors departed the East.

⊠ *Reichstagufer 17*
☎ *206 100*
🕐 *from 18:00 (box office)*
S-Bahn/U-Bahn: *Friedrichstraße*

National Opera House

The Staatsoper was Berlin's very first theatre and also the first building on what subsequently became known as the Forum Fridericianum. Designed by Georg von Knobelsdorff, it was completed in 1743. It was also the first important Berlin building to suffer serious wartime damage. With its neo-Classical gabled portico supported by six Corinthian columns, the clean-lined Staatsoper presents a pleasing architectural balance with the Alte Bibliothek.

⊠ *Unter den Linden 7*
☎ *203 540*
🕐 *Mon–Fri 11:00–19:00, Sat–Sun 14:00–19:00*
U-Bahn: *Hausvogteiplatz*

New Chancellery

The site is close to the western end of Leipziger Straße. Built in 1938 and housing Hitler's office, it stood at the junction of Wilhelmstraße and

Voss Straße; an apartment block and kindergarten are now on the site. To the west stood the Old Chancellery, in what for 28 years was the 'no-man's-land' of the Wall. Its garden contained Hitler's bunker, where the Führer spent the last six weeks of his life before committing suicide on 30 April 1945, blaming the German people for his failure to conquer Europe.

✉ *Wilhelmstraße*
U-Bahn: *Mohrenstraße*

Kaiser Wilhelm Memorial Church

The Kaiser-Wilhelm-Gedächtniskirche (Kaiser Wilhelm Memorial Church), with its bomb-shattered tower and spire, is an instantly recognizable symbol of Berlin. The neo-Romanesque church was built in 1895 as a memorial to Kaiser Wilhelm I, but fell victim to Allied bombing on 22 November 1943, which left just the severely damaged western end standing. The remains stand as a memorial both to the horrors of World War II and the devastation suffered by Berlin.

✉ *Breitscheidplatz*
☎ *218 5023*
🕐 *daily 09:00–19:00; guided tours Mon–Sat 13:15, 14:00, 15:00*
S-Bahn/U-Bahn: *Zoologischer Garten*

Wasserturm

Just south of Kollwitzplatz is a Prenzl'berg landmark – the fat, yellow-brick Wasserturm (Water Tower) on Knaackstraße, built in 1875. In use until 1915, it was taken over by the Nazis, who turned its basement into an interrogation and torture chamber. Now it is an oddly shaped apartment house – a protected building with a memorial stone that pays tribute to freedom fighters killed by the Nazis in 1933.

✉ *Knaackstraße*
U-Bahn: *Senefelderplatz*

Above: *The bomb-shattered spire of the Kaiser Wilhelm Memorial Church – a monument to the horrors of war.*

Below: *A sculpture of the prominent Berlin artist Käthe Kollwitz in Prenzlauer Berg.*

Neues Palais

Built by Friedrich II as a symbol of Prussian might in the aftermath of the successful Seven Years' War, the red-brick Neues Palais (New Palace) with its huge green dome was an extravagant addition to Park Sanssouci in 1769. A few of the palace's 200 or so rooms are on view to the public.

✉ *Potsdam*
☎ *0331 969 4202*
🕓 *Tue–Sun 09:00–17:00 (Apr–Oct), 09:00–16:00 (Nov–Mar)*
S-Bahn: *Potsdam Hauptbahnhof*

Museums and Galleries
Huguenot Museum and Library

The Französischer Dom was completed in 1705 as the church of the French Huguenots. It was designed on the lines of the Huguenots' own church in Charenton, with the dome by Karl von Gontard added in 1785. Today the Huguenot Museum, tracing their history in France and relocation to Berlin and Brandenburg, and the Huguenot Library occupy part of the ground floor.

✉ *Gendarmenmarkt*
☎ *229 1760*
🕓 *Tue–Sat 12:00–17:00, Sun 11:00–17:00*
U-Bahn: *Stadtmitte, Französische Straße*

Knoblauchhaus

The stuccoed Knoblauchhaus in Poststraße, once owned by the Knoblauch family (the family name means 'garlic'), is one of the Nikolaiviertel's only two genuine old buildings. Designed by Friedrich Wilhelm Dietrichs, it was completed in 1759 and amazingly survived World War II. The building is reopening in January 2007 and shows the lifestyle of a well-off 19th-century Berlin family, complete with art

works and period Biedermeier furniture.
✉ Poststraße 23
☎ 2345 9991
🕓 Tue, Thu–Sun 10:00–18:00, Wed 12:00–20:00
S-Bahn/U-Bahn: Alexanderplatz

Hanf Museum

The Hanf Museum (Hemp Museum) that opened in 1994 tells the history of hemp cultivation and its use in medicine, agriculture and building – also its cultural and religious uses and the legal implications involved.
✉ Mühlendamm
☎ 242 4827
🕓 Tue–Fri 10:00–20:00, Sat–Sun 12:00–20:00
S-Bahn/U-Bahn: Alexanderplatz

Käthe Kollwitz Museum

A collection of sculptures, drawings, prints and posters by Berlin's greatest female artist Käthe Kollwitz, many focusing on war and poverty, fills the restored 1870s villa.
✉ Fasanenstraße 24
☎ 882 5210
🕓 11:00–18:00, closed Tue; taped audio tours available
U-Bahn: Kurfürstendamm

Jüdisches Museum

The Jewish Museum, designed by Daniel Libeskind, includes the art and history collection previously on display in the Martin-Gropius-Bau and vividly portrays the life of Berlin's Jewish population. There were about 60,000 Jewish people living in Berlin at the outbreak of World War II, of whom 50,000 died in concentration camps.
✉ Lindenstraße 9-14
☎ 2599 3300
🕓 Mon 10:00–22:00, Tue–Sun 10:00–20:00; closed Jewish holidays
U-Bahn: Hallesches Tor

Gay Museum

Just north of Viktoria Park in Kreuzberg is one of those attractions to be found only in Berlin – the **Schwules Museum** (Gay Museum) – covering every aspect of homosexual life. The museum is funded by private donations.
✉ On the third floor in the second courtyard at Mehringdamm 61
☎ 6959 9050
🕓 Mon, Wed–Fri, Sun 14:00–18:00, Sat 14:00–19:00
U-Bahn: Mehringdamm

Places of Worship and Green Spaces
Neue Synagoge

Berlin's Jewish community is centred on Oranienburger Straße and the New Synagogue (Neue Synagoge), situated midway along the north side of the street. Designed by Eduard Knoblauch, it was built to hold a congregation of 3000. On Kristallnacht it was saved from being burned down by the action of local police chief Wilhelm Krützfeld, who successfully pleaded with Nazi thugs that the

Above: *The New Synagogue on Oranienburger Straße is the hub of Berlin's Jewish community.*

Views of Berlin
The best views of Berlin are to be had from the **Fernsehturm** (TV Tower) in the eastern city centre and the **Funkturm** (Radio Tower) at the Berlin Exhibition Grounds to the west. From the viewing gallery 200m (656ft) up the Fernsehturm (it translates as 'far-seeing tower'), on a clear day you can see 35km (22 miles) to the **countryside** beyond Berlin's borders. Closer to the tower you can identify the inner-city districts of Kreuzberg, Prenzlauer Berg and Friedrichshain. From the viewing gallery 130m (427ft) up the Funkturm there is a grand panorama of Berlin's **lake district** to the west of the city.

---

building was a national monument – a plaque on the wall commemorates his brave deed.

✉ *Oranienburger Straße*
☎ *880 28 316*
🕐 *There is a permanent exhibition open Sun–Thu 10:00–18:00, Fri 10:00–14:00*
S-Bahn: *Oranienburger Straße*

Volkspark Friedrichshain

Berlin's largest park, the Friedrichshain People's Park, was laid out in 1840 to mark the centenary of Friedrich II (Frederick the Great) assuming the throne. It is crisscrossed by good paths and provides a haven of welcome greenery in a heavily urbanized landscape. At the northwestern corner of the park is the delightful Märchenbrunnen (Fairytale Fountain) surrounded by characters taken from tales by the Brothers Grimm.

✉ *Am Friedrichshain*
U-Bahn: *Schillingstraße*

Treptower Park

In the centre of the 78ha (193-acre) Treptower Park, the Sowjetisches Ehrenmal (Soviet Monument) commemorates the lives of some 5000 of the Red Army soldiers killed in the Battle of Berlin in April–May 1945 – they are buried close by. The site contains a mausoleum, as well as an 11m (36ft) high monument, depicting a Soviet soldier carrying a child, his sword resting on a broken swastika.

✉ *Alt Treptow*
S-Bahn: *Treptower Park*

ACTIVITIES
Sport and Recreation

Berlin's bid to host the 2000 Olympic Games was an effort to eclipse the 1936 Games staged three years after the Nazis had seized power. The bid failed, but the city has pressed ahead with the creation of new sporting venues. The Velodrome now stages the Berlin six-day cycle race first held at Berlin Zoo in 1909, while the Max Schmeling Hall in Prenzlauer Berg is pulling in big crowds for its ice hockey and basketball events. The Berlin Marathon attracts a large entry in late summer. The modernized Hoppegarten racetrack stages horse-race meetings.

Cycling

Getting around Berlin by bike is easy as the city is flat, many roads are wide and most of the main arteries have their own cycle track – it is obligatory to use the cycle track if it is marked with the blue bicycle traffic sign. With Berlin's sights spread between Charlottenburg in the west and Mitte in the east, and further out to the suburbs, there are bicycle rental outlets throughout the city and you can even cycle the route of the Wall.

Sailing

With no fewer than 50 lakes and 200km (124 miles) of navigable rivers and canals, Berlin is an ideal city for sailing. The River Spree crosses the city from Grosser Müggelsee and the southeastern lakes; in the west the River Havel enters the

See Berlin by Bike
Berlin on Bike
⊠ Knackstraße 97
☎ 4404 8300
Guided bike tours on six routes, such as the Berlin Wall tour at 10:00 daily.

Zweit.rad Touren
⊠ Fehrbelliner Straße 82
☎ 5364 8289
Sightseeing tours of the Berlin highlights. Small groups are led by trained guides.

Berlin Starting Point
⊠ Bergmannstraße 104
☎ 6272 1303
Bike tours led by qualified guides.

Below: *Berlin is an ideal city to see on two wheels.*

Golf Courses
Berlin Wannsee
Golf Club
☎ 806 7060

Golfpark Schloß
Wilkendorf
☎ 03341 330 960

Berliner Golf Club
Gatow
☎ 365 7660

Global Golf Berlin
☎ 2269 7844
🕓 daily 07:00–22:00

Golfzentrum Berlin-
Mitte
☎ 2804 7070
🕓 daily 07:00–23:00

Wannsee lakes. Information on sailing in Berlin or on the surrounding waterways can be obtained from **Berliner Segler-Verband** (☎ 3083 9908). **The Berlin-Brandenburg Water Sports Association** (🖥 www.wtb-brb.de) issues a map of the waterways.

Golf

Golfers can take their clubs to Berlin knowing they will have somewhere to play close to the city. **Berlin Wannsee Golf Club** is in the Wannsee area, 17km (10 miles) from the city centre; **Golfpark Schloß Wilkendorf** has its championship-rated Sandy Lyle Course; and **Berliner Golf Club Gatow** is a nine-hole course 16km (9 miles) from the centre. You can still strike a golf ball without leaving the city – **Global Golf Berlin** is a first-class inner-city driving range complete with clubhouse and putting greens, while **Golfzentrum Berlin-Mitte** also has floodlit practice.

Ice Skating

Get your skates on and head for the **Eisstadion Berlin Wilmersdorf** in Wilmersdorf (☎ 8973 2734). There's an outer speed-skating circuit and an area for figure skating. The best-priced public ice rink in Berlin is the **Erika-Hess-Eisstadion** in Wedding, open until 22:00 on Fridays and Saturdays (☎ 200 945 550). The Christmas market in Alexanderplatz also has an ice rink.

Ice Hockey
Ice hockey is popular in Berlin and the giants of the game are the **Berlin Capitals** and **ECH Eisbären** teams. The Capitals are the old West Berlin team and the Eisbären hail from the former East Berlin, hence the ongoing rivalry between the two teams. The sport is now big business in Germany since the setting up of a national league.

Athletics

Athletes converge on Berlin each September to take part in the **Berlin Marathon** – the race draws 40,000 runners annually, starting at Charlottenburger Tor and finishing at the Kaiser-Wilhelm Gedächtniskirche.

The **Berlin Half-Marathon** takes place in April and the 10km (6-mile) **City Night Run** on the Ku'damm in August. Berlin is an excellent city for running in thanks to its many parks – a trot through a snow-covered Tiergarten on a chilly January morning will work up an appetite for breakfast.

Spectator Sports
Soccer in Berlin

Soccer is king in Germany (the West Germans have won the World Cup on three occasions) and **Hertha BSC** is the capital's leading club. In GDR days, Dynamo Berlin ruled the roost on the eastern side of the Wall, winning their own national championship no fewer than 10 times. In the face of competition from Hertha, the club dropped the state-backed 'Dynamo' prefix and adopted amateur status as **FC Berlin**. The Bundesliga cup finals held at the

Berlin Marathon
✉ Glockenturm 23
☎ 3012 8810
🖥 www.berlin-marathon.com
🕑 last Sun in Sep

Hertha Berlin Soccer Club
☎ 0180 518 9200
🖥 www.herthabsc.de

Below: Soccer fans celebrate a German victory in the World Cup.

Galopprennbahn-Hoppegarten
✉ Goetheallee 1,
Dahlwitz-Hoppegarten
☎ 0334 238 930
S-Bahn: Hoppegarten
⏱ racing Apr–Oct

Pferdesportpark
✉ Treskowallee 129,
Karlshorst
☎ 5001 7121
S-Bahn: Karlshorst
⏱ racing year-round
Wed at 18:00

Lenz
✉ Eisenacher Straße 3
☎ 217 7820

Hafen
✉ Motzstraße 19
☎ 211 4118

The Sharon Stonewall
✉ Linienstraße 136
☎ 2408 5502

Möbel Olfe
✉ Reichenberger Straße 177
☎ 6165 9612

Christopher Street Day Parade
☎ 2362 8632

Gay and Lesbian Run
☎ 445 7561

Lesbian Film Festival
☎ 7871 8109

Opposite: *The imposing entrance to Berlin Zoo.*

Olympic Stadium pull in crowds of 75,000 each year. The venue was given a costly facelift for the **2006 World Cup Finals** staged in Germany – it hosted the final of the tournament between Italy and France.

Horse Racing

Horse racing aficionados are catered for in Berlin at the popular **Galopprennbahn-Hoppegarten**, which dates back to 1867. Trotting events are held at the **Pferdesportpark** – the only trotting venue in the old GDR, dating from 1862 – and the **Trabrennbahn Mariendorf**, founded in 1913, where the August Derby Week is an important international meeting.

American Football

Berlin Thunder is one of the big teams in the NFL Europe – they won the World Bowl in 2001, 2002 and 2004 and reached the final in 2005. The season runs from late March/early April until the end of May; Berlin Thunder's home games are at the Olympic Stadium.

Alternative Berlin

Berlin's reputation as the European centre of the gay lifestyle dates from the 1920s, when clubs like the Eldorado and Kleist-Casino were venues for the city's gay and lesbian groups. Today more than 100 gay bars flourish in Berlin, many of them around Nollendorfplatz in Schöneberg, a few blocks south of the Tiergarten; among the more popular gay bars are **Lenz**, **Hafen**, the **Sharon Stonewall** and **Möbel Olfe** in the Oranienstraße neighbourhood.

Berlin's large gay population suffered persecution under the Nazis and a considerable number were dispatched to concentration camps – a triangular plaque in the wall outside Nollendorfplatz U-Bahn station recalls the plight of interred gays who were forced to wear the Pink Triangle in the camps. Berlin resumed its role as a mecca for gays in the 1960s and is today recognized as one of the world's most gay-friendly cities.

The **Christopher Street Day Parade**, originally organized to commemorate the Stonewall Bar riots on New York's Christopher Street in 1969, is Berlin's biggest gay gathering by far, with up to 400,000 people taking to the streets. The huge party takes place in June/July, with wacky costumes and rainbow flags to the fore. Other gay-related events include the **Gay and Lesbian Run** which takes place on alternate years in May, and the **Lesbian Film Festival** in October.

Kids' Delight

City breaks can be fun for the children, too. Take them to the **Berlin Zoo** at the Tiergarten and introduce them to its stars, the cute pandas Bao Bao and Yan Yan, or the **Tierpark Berlin** in Lichtenberg, the city's second zoo. In the **Märkisches Museum**, they will enjoy the noisy display of 18th-century mechanical instruments called automatones. Pressing buttons at the **Deutsches Technikmuseum** will amuse them for hours, as will the museum's Science Center Spectrum building, designed for experimentation. In the **Museum für Naturkunde** they will wonder at the scale of the

Berlin Zoo
✉ Hardenbergplatz 8
🕐 Mar–Oct 09:00–18:30, Oct–Mar 09:00–17:00
💰 10 euro

Tierpark Berlin
✉ Am Tierpark 125
🕐 09:00–16:00/19:00
💰 10 euro

Märkisches Museum
✉ Am Köllnisches Park 5
🕐 Tue, Thu–Sun 10:00–18:00, Wed 12:00–20:00
💰 4 euro

Deutsches Technikmuseum
✉ Trebbiner Straße 9
🕐 Tue–Fri 09:00–17:30, Sat–Sun 10:00–18:00
💰 4.50 euro

Museum für Naturkunde
✉ Invalidenstraße 43
🕐 Tue–Fri 09:30–17:00, Sat–Sun 10:00–18:00
💰 3.50 euro

Above: *A puppet seller attracts a youngster's attention in the western city centre.*

dinosaurs on display when the Dinosaur Hall reopens in 2007. Among the exhibits is the largest exhibited skeleton of a dinosaur, the Brachiosaurus.

Southern Fun

Head for the southern districts of Neukölln and Treptow for some off-centre leisure venues. The **Blub Badeparadies** at Buschkrugallee 64 in Neukölln is one of Europe's most attractive and varied water parks, while the **Stadtbad Neukölln** at Ganghoferstraße 3–5 was described as Europe's most beautiful indoor swimming pool when it opened in 1914. The **Spree-Park Berlin** at Neue Krugallee in Treptow contains one of Europe's biggest loop-the-loops, a Ferris wheel providing a fantastic view of the city, 30 carousels, a helter-skelter, amphitheatre and western-style Colorado City attraction.

Guided Walks

While many of Berlin's main sights can be seen from the comfort of an air-conditioned tour bus, by far the best way to discover the city is on foot. Regular guided walks take place throughout the city, each dwelling on a particular theme, with titles such as: 'Through the Wild East with Franz Bieberkopf', 'Alexanderplatz, the Rough Heart of Berlin', 'The Kreuzberg Experience' and 'Oases in a City Desert'. The walks have become popular with residents and visitors alike – the Berlin Tourist Office can help with details. Whether you want to be guided through Mitte, the old heart of East Berlin, or Charlottenburg, its former West Berlin counterpart, setting out on foot is the way to really capture the atmosphere of the city. And there are neighbourhoods like Kreuzberg and Prenzlauer Berg (*see* below) to discover too.

Prenzl'berg Walk (*see* Map G)

This short walk takes you around the heart of the Prenzlauer Berg district. Take the U-Bahn to Senefelderplatz. Turn right up the wide Schönhauser Allee to the Jüdischer Friedhof (Jewish Cemetery). Continue past the cemetery and take the first right into Wörther Straße. Proceed to Kollwitzplatz. Midway along the north side of the park at Restauration 1900, turn left into Husemann-straße. Take the first right into Sredzkistraße and then right again into Kollwitzstraße returns you to Kollwitzplatz. At the southern tip of the square turn left into Knaack-straße. Turn right past the Wasserturm (Water Tower), and then left at the end to emerge on wide Prenzlauerallee. Catch a tram back to Hackescher Markt.

Organized Tours

The majority of Berlin sightseeing tours are of the 'hop on, hop off' variety, such as City Circle Sightseeing operated by **Berolina**. You pay an all-day or half-day fare (20 or 15 euro in Berolina's case) and get on and off as many times as you wish at any of the 15 stops. Buses leave every 15 minutes and there is a choice of eight languages. **Top Tour Berlin** has open-top double-deckers operating a similar route every 20 minutes, while **Severin + Kuhn** and **Zille Bus** (with vintage 'Roaring Twenties'-style buses) are other operators.

Original Berlin Walks
☎ 301 9194
🖳 www.berlinwalks.com
Pioneered historical guided walking tours in the early 1990s. Regular tours (in English) include Discover Berlin (the main sights), Infamous Third Reich Sites, Sachsenhausen Concentration Camp Memorial Tour, Jewish Life in Berlin, and Discover Postdam.

Brewer's Best of Berlin
☎ 0177 3881 537
🖳 www.brewers berlintours.com
Offers an all-day Berlin Walking Tour, a shorter Classic Berlin Tour, private Cold War tours, a Third Reich Tour, and a Nightlife Tour.

Berlin Sightseeing Tours
☎ 7974 5600
🖳 www.berlin-sightseeing-tours.de
Offers guided walks of various durations for pre-booked groups.

Berolina Sightseeing
☎ 8856 8030

Top Tour Berlin
☎ 0185 443 188

Severin + Kuhn
☎ 880 4190

Zille Bus
☎ 2652 5569

Botanical Garden

✉ Königin-Luise-
Straße 6-8

☎ 8385 0100

🕐 garden daily 09:00
to dusk; museum daily
09:00–16:00 Nov–Jan,
09:00 to dusk Feb–Oct

💰 5 euro (combined)

S-Bahn: Botanischer
Garten

Bicycle Tours

If walking Berlin's
streets on your sight-
seeing mission starts
wearing thin, hire a
bike and pedal off
through the Tiergarten.
The chief bike rental
shop in Berlin is
Fahrradstation

☎ 0180 510 8000

🕐 Mon–Fri
10:00–19:00, Sat
10:00–15:00/16:00
New branch at:

✉ Friedrichstraße 95

🕐 Mar–Oct from
08:00–20:00

Below: *The Botanical
Garden at Dahlem.*

Flower Power

More than 20,000 plant species from all corners of the globe have a home in Berlin's luxuriant **Botanical Garden** at Dahlem to the southwest of the city. Covering 43ha (106 acres), it is one of the largest in the world and contains a 'touch' garden for the visually handicapped. You can spend hours admiring the amazing displays and then increase your knowledge of the subject in the **Botanisches Museum** within the grounds, where the history of plants and their current distribution are explained. Exhibits include dioramas of different vegetation types and grain from ancient Egyptian burial sites.

Beach Break

When you feel like a break from the city, Wannsee beckons. Here you will find Europe's largest inland beach, with boats and pedaloes for hire – there's even a nudist beach. Boat trips operate from Wannsee to **Pfaueninsel** (Peacock Island), where Friedrich Wilhelm II had a small folly built for his mistress Wilhelmine Encke in 1794–97; within it is a small museum. The **Haus der Wannsee Konferenz** (Wannsee Conference Building) is an exclusive villa in which Nazi leaders planned the mass extermination of countless European Jews in January 1942, in what was later to become known as the Final Solution.

Left: *Shopping in the dramatically designed Galeries Lafayette can be quite an experience.*

Shopping

Berlin would take quite some beating for the quality of its shopping. Tourists generally make a leisurely stroll down **Kurfürstendamm** a priority, if only to window-gaze at the vast array of quality goods for sale in the shops. But nowadays the city's number one shopping street is facing some tough competition from other parts of the city – from the new gallery at **Potsdamer Platz** and also from the still evolving **Friedrichstraße**. And those visitors who prefer to avoid the shopping crowds will still be able to find an excellent selection of stylish individual shops in the **Hackesche Höfe** area of the city.

Shopping Centres
KaDeWe (KDW)

Short for Kaufhaus des Westens, Europe's largest department store appears to sell just about everything you can imagine. The six-storey emporium was built in 1906 and includes its famous food floor, a conservatory restaurant and

> **Old is New**
> The new word in German retail is 'Ostalgia' – a hankering after anything to do with the former East Gemany. **East Berlin**, ✉ Kastanienallee 13, ☎ 534 4042, is good for clothes with Ostalgia flair, while **Berlin Story**, ✉ Unter den Linden 40, ☎ 2045 3840, has worthwhile GDR souvenirs. **Ampelmännchen Galerie**, ✉ Hackesche Höfe, sells items carrying the symbolic red and green traffic light men of the old GDR.

Stilwerk

Top names in international design can be found in Stilwerk, four floors dedicated to interior design. They include **Bang & Olufsen**, **Gaggenau** and **Leonardo**. The jazz club **Soultrane** is also here.

✉ Kantstraße 17
☎ 3151 5500
🕓 Mon–Sat 10:00–20:00
S-Bahn: Savignyplatz

New Kranziereck

New Kranziereck is a new shopping development on Kurfürstendamm built around the legendary **Café Kranzler**. The high glass tower block has attracted many boutiques and well-known clothing brands.

✉ Kurfürstendamm 24
🕓 Mon–Sat 10:00–20:00
U-Bahn: Kurfürstendamm

glass panorama lift. All but destroyed in World War II, it was rebuilt in the 1950s and grew in stature to become a symbol of the free-market economy.

✉ Tauentzienstraße 21-24, ☎ 21 21-0, 🕓 Mon–Fri 10:00–20:00, Sat 09:30–20:00, **U-Bahn:** Wittenbergplatz

Europa-Center

Right across Tauentzienstraße from KDW, this is an indoor shopping complex on two floors enhanced by its original Flow of Time Clock and pleasant interior water garden. Built in 1965, it was the first shopping mall in the city and has around 100 shops.

✉ Tauentzienstraße 9, ☎ 2649 7940, **U-Bahn:** Kurfürstendamm

Potsdamer Platz

Here the split-level **Arkaden** offers all kinds of shops, prominent among them those selling shoes, textiles and design objects.

✉ Alte Potsdamer Straße 7, ☎ 2559 2714, 🕓 Mon–Sat 10:00–20:00, **S-Bahn/U-Bahn:** Potsdamer Platz

Shopping Streets
Ku'damm

The Kurfürstendamm is crammed with department stores, high-fashion shops and boutiques – along with several cinemas and a good few restaurants in which to recover from the activity of the buying spree. Off the Ku'damm, situated along side streets such as Fasanenstraße and Bleibtreustraße, are the most expensive fashion houses: big names represented here include **Jil Sander**, **Rene Lezard**, **Prada**, **Zegna** and **Windsor**. Here, too, are top jewellers **Cartier** and **Tiffany**. Also on the Ku'damm is a **Meissen** shop selling the expensive German porcelain (there is another on Unter den Linden).

U-Bahn: Kurfürstendamm

Friedrichstraße

The many new buildings on Friedrichstraße include the Friedrichstadtpassagen, with boutiques and restaurants prominent. Galeries Lafayette (see below) is in Quarter 207, while the connecting Quarter 206 houses boutiques of many top designers in Art Deco style.

S-Bahn/U-Bahn: *Friedrichstraße*

Hackesche Höfe Boutiques

Hackesche Höfe consists of eight courtyards that have been expertly restored and now include a selection of smaller shops and galleries.

⊠ *Rosenthaler Straße 40/41,* ☎ *2809 8010,* ⊕ *shop hours vary,* **U-Bahn:** *Hackescher Markt*

Shops
Galeries Lafayette

The impressive design of architect Jean Nouvel sets Galeries Lafayette apart – it has an all-glass façade

and an atrium that tapers downwards to the basement food hall. There are three floors of designer wear and accessories.

⊠ *Friedrichstraße 76,* ☎ *209 480,* ⊕ *Mon–Sat 10:00–20:00,* **U-Bahn:** *Französische Straße*

The British Bookshop

Near the former Checkpoint Charlie, it's well stocked with British and American books, newspapers and magazines.

⊠ *Mauerstraße 83–84,* ☎ *238 4680,* ⊕ *Mon–Fri 10:00–18:00, Sat 10:00–16:00,* **U-Bahn:** *Kochstraße*

Kaufhof

The large 1970s-built store fronting the

Schöneberg Shops

The southern district of Schöneberg boasts a variety of retail outlets with a difference:

Bruno's
⊠ Bülowstraße 106
☎ 2147 3293
A gay-themed shop.

Körpernam
⊠ Maassenstraße 8
☎ 215 7471
A trendy little lingerie shop.

Luccico
⊠ Goltzstraße 34
☎ 216 6517
The place to go for top Italian shoes.

Vampyr De Luxe
⊠ Goltzstraße 39
☎ 217 2038
Has a good range of designer clothes and accessories.

Below: *Souvenirs of the former East German state are a popular buy.*

Above: *The Arkaden shopping mall, with more than 100 shops, is a focal point of the Potzdamer Platz area.*

Art Galleries
Take your pick of art galleries in Berlin:

Galerie Brockstedt
✉ Mommsenstraße 59
☎ 885 0500
A gallery respected for the work of contemporary masters.

Galerie Michael Schultz
✉ Mommsenstraße 34
☎ 324 1591
Features the work of German painters and sculptors.

Two Mitte galleries are:

Galerie Eigen & Art
✉ Auguststraße 26
☎ 280 6605

Galerie Wohnmaschine
✉ Tucholskystraße 35
☎ 3087 2015

---

wide expanse of Alexanderplatz has now lost its distinctive façade. It was the big store of the former East Berlin; now, having undergone a major renovation, it's a typical westernized emporium selling a wide range of goods.
✉ *Alexanderplatz 9,*
☎ *247 430,* ⏰ *Mon–Sat 09:00–20:00,*
S-Bahn/U-Bahn: *Alexanderplatz*

Wertheim

In a prominent position on the Ku'damm, Wertheim is one of the chain stores. Goods are well presented and the store is noted for its menswear.
✉ *Kurfürstendamm 231,* ☎ *880 030,*
⏰ *Mon–Sat 10:00–20:00,* **U-Bahn:** *Kurfürstendamm*

Zweitausendeins

This is the Berlin outlet of an online store with excellent discounts on new books, CDs, DVDs and videos. Excellent selection of classical, jazz and rock.
✉ *Kantstraße 41,*
☎ *312 5017,* ⏰ *Mon–Wed 10:00–19:00, Thu–Fri 10:00–20:00, Sat 10:00–16:00,* **U-Bahn:** *Wilmersdorfer Straße*

Meissener Porzellan

Meissen porcelain, from a town in the former GDR, is much sought-after with a price tag to match. Each item is handmade and hand-painted, with bowls, tablewear, vases and more, plus the ubiquitous figurines.
✉ *Unter den Linden 39B,* ☎ *2267 9028,*
⏰ *Mon–Fri 10:00–20:00, Sat 10:00–18:00,* **U-Bahn:** *Französische Straße*

Dussmann – Das Kulturkaufhaus

Big retail outlet on four floors, strong on books, CDs, DVDs and

videos. There are Internet terminals and an interactive video-viewing room.
✉ *Friedrichstraße 90,* ☎ *2025 2400,* ⏰ *Mon–Sat 10:00–22:00,* **S-Bahn/U-Bahn:** *Friedrichstraße*

Markets

Visit Berlin just before Christmas and the aroma of mulled wine, candied almonds and cinnamon cakes is never far away: this is the season when *Weihnachtsmärkte* (**Christmas markets**) spring up all over the city, their attractively decorated stalls packed with seasonal offerings. The most popular Christmas market is right beneath the Kaiser Wilhelm Memorial Church on **Breitscheidplatz;** the largest is in the Altstadt (old town) of **Spandau,** out to the northwest. Other markets are held at **Alexanderplatz,** on **Unter den Linden** and in **Sophienstraße** on the Scheunenviertel.

A **second-hand book mart** is held from time to time outside Humboldt University on Unter den Linden.

Big Berlin Junk and Art Market

Berlin's biggest and most popular art and flea market.
✉ *Straße des 17 Juni,* ⏰ *Sat and Sun 10:00–17:00,* **S-Bahn:** *Tiergarten*

Berlin Antiques and Flea Market

Recommended for collectors of curios and antiques.
✉ *in the S-Bahn arches at Georgen-straße near Friedrich-straße station,* ⏰ *daily 11:00–18:00 except Tue,* **S-Bahn/U-Bahn:** *Friedrichstraße*

Berlin Art and Nostalgia Market

A colourful market selling art, books, furniture and GDR 'souvenirs'.
✉ *on Museums Island,* ⏰ *Sat and Sun 11:00–17:00,* **S-Bahn/U-Bahn:** *Friedrichstraße*

Berlin Designers
Claudia Skoda is synonymous with Berlin designer clothing and her shop at ✉ Alte Schönhauser Straße 35, ☎ 280 7211, features her signature knitwear items. There is another Claudia Skoda shop at ✉ Linienstraße 156. Local design also has an outlet in **Tagebau**, at ✉ Rosenthaler Straße 19 – it's a co-operative of Berlin designers that also retails furniture and home accessories. **Molotow**, at ✉ Gneisenaustraße 112 in Kreuzberg, is another outlet for Berlin fashion.

Youth Hostels
Jugendherberge Am Wannsee
☎ 803 2304
On the edge of the Grunewald forest.

Jugendherberge Ernst Reuter
☎ 404 1610
In the northern Reinickendorf district.

Jugendherberge Berlin International
☎ 261 1097
Near the Tiergarten park in the city centre.

Camping
The German Camping Club
✉ Mandlstraße 28, 80802 Munich
☎ 00 49 89 380 1420
🖵 wwwcamping-club.de

Below: *The Bristol Hotel Kempinski, on the Ku'damm for half a century.*

WHERE TO STAY

Before selecting your hotel, decide whether you want to stay in the western or eastern part of the city – that is, in the vicinity of the Ku'damm shopping and nightlife area, or close to the historical sights. In the west, there is a wider choice of all kinds of accommodation, from the simple pensions between the Ku'damm and Kantstraße to five-star grandeur around the Tiergarten – the legacy of pre-unification days. Nevertheless, since 1989 there has been considerable hotel investment in the former East Berlin and many international hotel chains are now represented in that part of the city. The **Berlin Tourism** hotline, ☎ +49 (0) 30 25 00 25, 🖶 +49 (0) 30 25 00 24 24, can be used to book your accommodation – from a room in a luxury hotel to a bed in a youth hostel – before you leave home or on arrival in Berlin. The line is open Monday–Friday 08:00–20:00, Saturday–Sunday and public holidays 09:00–18:00. If you are telephoning the hotel direct from outside Berlin, the city code for all the properties listed is (030).

The majority of hotels in the mid- and upper ranges have their own websites, and in many cases you can make a direct booking. There are also a number of booking agencies (with their own websites) that give you information about hotels you are interested in and allow you to make reservations online.

Websites are also good for checking out the availability of hotel deals – many Berlin properties offer good weekend deals, especially at the top end of the market where hotels are used mainly by business people during weekdays.

Lower down the price scale, the bed and breakfast concept is catching on fast in German cities and good-value accommodation can be found in the Pension type of property – the district of Charlottenburg is noted for its wide selection.

Hotels are concentrated in Mitte in the eastern part of Berlin and in the districts of Charlottenburg and Tiergarten in the west of the city.

Since the fall of the Wall in 1989, the range of options in the east of the city has increased enormously, from trendy backpacker hostels to the utmost in luxury.

In the last 15 years the number of visitor beds in Berlin has tripled to approximately the 80,000 mark, with new properties being added regularly.

There are three official youth hostels in Berlin, all members of the **German Youth Hostels Association** (DJH). They tend to fill up quickly, so it is wise to book well in advance. Camping is an option in Berlin, but there are no sites close to the city centre (*see* panel, page 54).

Consider These

As an alternative to bedding down in the centre of Berlin, consider a hotel in the characterful districts of Prenzlauer Berg or Kreuzberg. One of the best properties in **Prenzlauer Berg** is **Ackselhaus**, ✉ Belforter Straße 21, ☎ 4433 7633, with rooms and apartments available on a charming residential street; the apartments sleep up to four. Less expensive options include the small **Hotel Greifswald**, ✉ Greifswalder Straße 211, ☎ 443 5283, with summer breakfasts in the courtyard, and **Myer's Hotel**, ✉ Metzer Straße 26, ☎ 440 140.

In **Kreuzberg**, the intimate 12-room **Hotel Riehmers Hofgarten**, ✉ Yorckstraße 83, ☎ 7809 8800, is in a restored 1891 courtyard building, and the **Pension Kreuzberg**, ✉ Grossbeerenstraße 64, ☎ 251 1362, provides an inexpensive stay.

Eastern City

• *LUXURY*

Adlon Kempinski

(Map D–F3)

This hotel was opened in 1997 near the Brandenburg Gate on the site of the original Adlon, which was built in 1907 and then destroyed in World War II. With its 337 rooms, it is the last word in luxury.

✉ *Unter den Linden 77, 10117 Berlin-Mitte,* ☎ *226 10,* 🕾 *2261 2222.*

Albrechtshof

(Map D–F2)

Luxury hotel with its own chapel in the government quarter. Breakfast can be taken in the courtyard garden and the restaurant offers traditional Berlin cuisine.

✉ *Albrechtstraße 8, 10117 Berlin-Mitte,* ☎ *308 860,* 🕾 *3088 6100.*

Alexander Plaza Berlin (Map D–H2)

In the midst of Mitte, this renovated 92-room hotel qualifies for the 'boutique' tag, with a bright colour scheme and modern furniture. The Wintergarten restaurant is in a central courtyard.

✉ *Rosenstraße 1, 10178 Berlin-Mitte,* ☎ *240 010,* 🕾 *2400 1777.*

Dorint Sofitel

(Map D–F3)

Stylish top-end hotel with fewer than 100 rooms. It includes a spa with steam bath, sauna and great views over Gendarmenmarkt. A popular property, so obtaining one of the (expensive) rooms may not be easy.

✉ *Charlottenstraße 50-52, 10117 Berlin-Mitte,* ☎ *203 750,* 🕾 *2037 5100.*

Hilton (Map D–G3)

Right on historic Gendarmenmarkt, the 354-room Hilton opened in 1991. Hilton was one of the first international chains to expand into Berlin after the collapse of the Wall.

✉ *Mohrenstraße 30, 10117 Berlin-Mitte,* ☎ *202 30,* 🕾 *2023 4269.*

Maritim ProArte

(Map D–F2)

The German hotel chain's 1990s property has 403 rooms and is situated two minutes' walk from Friedrichstraße rail station.

✉ *Friedrichstraße 151, 10117 Berlin-Mitte,* ☎ *203 35,* 🕾 *2033 4209.*

Radisson SAS

(Map D–G2)

An impressive new build, it faces the Dom across the River Spree. In the atrium-lobby is a 25m (80ft) high aquarium with 2500 fish varieties.

✉ *Karl-Liebknecht Straße 5, 10178 Berlin-Mitte,* ☎ *238 280,* 🕾 *238 2810.*

Regent Berlin

(Map D–F3)

This is an excellent five-star hotel with 195 rooms and a well-deserved outstanding reputation. It is situated close to the Gendarmenmarkt.

✉ *Charlottenstraße 49, 10117 Berlin-Mitte,* ☎ *203 38,* 🕾 *2033 6119.*

Westin Grand

(Map D–F3)

The Westin Grand opened its doors in 1987 and, during the two years before the Wall came down, established itself as East Berlin's best hotel. Still elegant, the 358-room hotel is now part of the Westin chain. ⊠ Friedrichstraße 158–164, 10117 Berlin-Mitte, ☎ 202 70, 📠 2027 3362.

MID-RANGE

Allegra (Map D–F2)

This modern 79-room hotel is housed in a 140-year-old building and situated close to the theatre district. ⊠ Albrechtstraße 17, 10117 Berlin-Mitte, ☎ 308 86 610, 📠 308 86 100.

Am Anhalter Bahnhof (Map D–F5)

This simply furnished small hotel is conveniently situated for the new Potsdamer Platz development. ⊠ Stresemannstraße 36, 10963 Berlin-Kreuzberg, ☎ 251 0342, 📠 251 4897.

Am Scheunen-viertel (Map D–G2)

Small 18-room hotel in the Jewish quarter of Oranienburger Straße and well placed for Museums Island and Friedrichstraße. ⊠ Oranienburger Straße 38, 10117 Berlin-Mitte, ☎ 282 2125, 📠 282 1115.

Art'otel Berlin Mitte (Map D–H3)

Superbly blends the old Ermelerhaus with modern architecture on the banks of the Spree. The hotel show-cases the work of artist Georg Baselitz, with original pieces on display in rooms and corridors. ⊠ Wallstraße 70-73, 10179 Berlin-Mitte, ☎ 240 620, 📠 2406 2222.

Honigmond

(Map D–F1)

Sister to the Honigmond Garden Hotel, it dates from 1899 and has been expertly renovated. It has just 40 rooms, half of which were added in 2004, and offers some of the best eastern city value. ⊠ Tieckstraße 12, 10115 Berlin-Mitte, ☎ 284 4550, 📠 2844 5511.

Ibis Berlin Mitte

(Map D–H1)

Typical modern Ibis hotel with 198 rooms, situated just a short tram ride away from the main city sights. ⊠ Prenzlauer Allee 4, 10405 Berlin-Prenzlauer Berg, ☎ 443 330, 📠 4433 3111.

Kastanienhof

(Map E–F3)

This is a smart 35-room hotel-pension. It is conveniently situated between the city centre and Prenzlauer Berg. ⊠ Kastanienallee 65, 10119 Berlin-Mitte, ☎ 443 050, 📠 4430 5111.

Park Inn Berlin

(Map D–H2)

With its 1006 rooms on 30 floors, the for-mer Hotel Stadt Berlin is Berlin's largest hotel

by far. The views over the city are excellent.
✉ *Alexanderplatz, 10178 Berlin-Mitte,*
☎ *238 90,*
🖷 *2389 4305.*

Unter den Linden
(Map D–F3)
Superbly situated on the corner of Unter den Linden and Friedrichstraße, this spruced-up relic of the GDR is unbeatable for convenience.
✉ *Unter den Linden 14, 10115 Berlin-Mitte,* ☎ *238 110,*
🖷 *2381 1100.*

• BUDGET
Aacron (Map D–F1)
The Aacron is a comfortable 21-room 'discount hotel'.
✉ *Friedrichstraße 124, 10117 Berlin-Mitte,* ☎ *282 9352,*
🖷 *280 8057.*

Artist Hotel-Pension Die Loge
(Map D–F2)
Cosy pension with just seven rooms.
✉ *Friedrichstraße 115, 10117 Berlin-Mitte,* ☎/🖷 *280 7513.*

Circus Hostel
(Map D–H1)
Two properties in fact – the Circus @ Rosa in Rosa-Luxemburg-Straße and the Circus @ Weinbergsweg, both within easy reach of Mitte's top sights.
✉ *Rosa-Luxemburg-Straße 39, 10178 Berlin-Mitte; Weinbergsweg 1A, 10119 Berlin-Mitte,* ☎ *2839 1433,* 🖷 *2839 1484.*

Citystay Hostel
(Map D–H2)
Spacious rooms for one to six people and dorm rooms with up to eight beds in this modern hostel which opened in 2005. Nice location on a quiet, traffic-free street.
✉ *Rosenstraße 16, 10718 Berlin-Mitte,* ☎ *2362 4031.*

Fabrik-Hostel Kreuzberg
(Map D–I4)
Inexpensive hostel in east Kreuzberg.
✉ *Schlesische Straße 18, 10997 Berlin-Kreuzberg,* ☎ *611 7116,* 🖷 *618 2974.*

Juncker's Hotel Garni (Map D–I2)
Tastefully furnished 30-room budget hotel just east of city centre.
✉ *Grünberger Straße 21, 10243 Berlin-Friedrichshain,* ☎ *293 3550,* 🖷 *2933 5555.*

baxpax downtown Hostel Hotel
(Map D–E1)
New sister establishment of Mitte's Backpacker Hostel. It has great facilities, including a lounge with fireplace.
✉ *Ziegelstraße 28, 10117 Berlin-Mitte,* ☎ *2787 4880,*
🖷 *2787 48899.*

Transit (Map D–F6)
Popular west Kreuzberg budget hotel.
✉ *Hagelberger Straße 53–54, 10965 Berlin-Kreuzberg,* ☎ *789 0470,*
🖷 *7890 4777.*

Western City
• LUXURY
Berlin Marriott
(Map D–E4)
It opened in early 2004 in the new Berlin

area of Potsdamer Platz. With just under 400 rooms and suites, the Berlin Marriott has made a big impression with business visitors to the German capital.
⊠ Inge-Beisheim-Platz 1, 10785 Berlin-Tiergarten,
☎ 220 000,
✆ 22000 1000.

Crowne Plaza Berlin City Centre
(Map D–B4)
The Crowne Plaza is a four-star-plus hotel situated near Berlin's big shops – KaDeWe et al.
⊠ Nürnberger Straße 65, 10787 Berlin-Schöneberg, ☎ 210 070, ✆ 213 2009.

Grand Hotel Esplanade
(Map D–D4)
There's an impressive entrance and lobby at this top-rated luxury hotel by the Landwehr Canal and close to the Tiergarten. The hotel's triangular swimming pool is a feature.
⊠ Lützowufer 15, 10785 Berlin-

Tiergarten, ☎ 254 780, ✆ 254 788 222.

Grand Hyatt Berlin (Map D–E4)
Classy five-star hotel, with 340 rooms. Handy for corporate executives doing business around high-rise Potsdamer Platz, but leisure guests may feel the ultramodern surroundings lack a true Berlin identity.
⊠ Marlene-Dietrich-Platz 2, 10785 Berlin-Tiergarten,
☎ 2553 1234,
✆ 2553 1235.

Inter-Continental
(Map D–C4)
Berlin's largest five-star hotel – it has 511 rooms – with the city's largest conference centre. It is especially popular with business guests.
⊠ Budapester Straße 2, 10787 Berlin-Tiergarten, ☎ 260 20, ✆ 2602 2600.

Kempinski Bristol Berlin (Map D–A4)
Opened in 1952, 'The Bristol' with its 301

The Friedrichshain District
For aesthetic Berlin without the sophistication of Charlottenburg or a revived Mitte, book yourself into the Friedrichshain district. The **East Side Hotel**, ⊠ Mühlenstraße 6, ☎ 293 833, is a modest property with views of the old Berlin Wall in the East Side Gallery. **Eastern Comfort**, ⊠ Mühlenstraße 73-77, ☎ 6676 3806, provides boat accommodation on the Spree – all the rooms have their own shower and toilet.

Share a House
If you are in Berlin for a longer stay, agencies can find you a room in a shared house or a furnished apartment. **Erste Mitwohnzentrale**, ☎ 324 3031, and **Wohn-Agentur Freiraum**, ☎ 618 2008, can both help in this respect, as can **Zeitraum Wohnkonzepte**, ☎ 441 6622. Prices are higher in the central districts, including Kreuzberg, Prenzlauer Berg and Schöneberg.

rooms thrives on its fashionable Ku'damm address.

✉ Kurfürstendamm 27, 10719 Berlin-Charlottenburg, ☎ 884 340, ✆ 883 6075.

Palace (Map D–B4)

The Palace is situated opposite the zoo and next door to the Europa-Center indoor shopping complex; guests at the 282-room hotel may use the adjacent health spa and sauna.

✉ Im Europa-Center, 10789 Berlin-Charlottenburg, ☎ 250 20, ✆ 2502 1197.

Ritz-Carlton

(Map D–E4)

A great place to be pampered after trekking round the sights. Built in 2004, it leans to Art Deco in style and has an outstanding restaurant where the service is second to none.

✉ Potsdamer Platz 3, 10785 Berlin-Tiergarten, ☎ 337 777, ✆ 33777 5555.

Schloßhotel im Grunewald

(Map E–E3)

Built as a Grunewald mansion for the aristocracy in 1912, the 52-room hotel offers Berlin's top luxury, as well as Berlin's top prices. The interior was designed by Karl Lagerfeld.

✉ Brahmsstraße 10, 14193 Berlin-Wilmersdorf, ☎ 895 840, ✆ 8958 4800.

• MID-RANGE

Am Zoo (Map D–A4)

Right on the Ku'damm, this hotel's 136 rooms provide welcome rest for visiting shopaholics.

✉ Kurfürstendamm 25, 10719 Berlin-Charlottenburg, ☎ 884 370, ✆ 8843 7714.

Best Western Kanthotel

(Map D–A4)

This popular 70-room hotel is a member of the Best Western chain.

✉ Kantstraße 111, 10627 Berlin-Charlottenburg, ☎ 323 020, ✆ 324 0952.

Charlottenburger Hof (Map E–E3)

Tidy 45-room hotel opposite Charlottenburg station.

✉ Stuttgarter Platz 14, 10627 Berlin-Charlottenburg, ☎ 329 070, ✆ 323 3723.

Golden Tulip Berlin Hotel Hamburg

(Map D–C4)

This well-priced 240-room hotel is convenient for KaDeWe and other large shops.

✉ Landgrafenstraße 4, 10787 Berlin-Tiergarten, ☎ 264 770, ✆ 262 9394.

Ibis Berlin Messe

(Map E–E3)

A 191-room chain hotel, handy for the ICC conference centre.

✉ Messedamm 10, 14057 Berlin-Charlottenburg, ☎ 303 930, ✆ 301 9536.

Savoy (Map D–A4)

This is a good-quality, 125-room hotel in the mid-priced range.

✉ Fasanenstraße 9–10, 10623 Berlin-

Charlottenburg,
☎ *311 030,*
📠 *3110 3333.*

• **BUDGET**
Haus der Begegnung
(Map D–B6)
Well-priced hotel two U-Bahn stops south of the Ku'damm.
✉ *Landhausstraße 10, 10717 Berlin-Wilmersdorf,*
☎ *860 0980,*
📠 *861 1758.*

Hotel-Pension Alexandra
(Map D–A5)
This small pension is situated just off the Ku'damm.
✉ *Wielandstraße 32, 10629 Berlin-*

Charlottenburg,
☎ *881 2107,*
📠 *8857 7818.*

Hotel-Pension Charlottenburg
(Map D–A4)
A simple and inexpensive establishment.
✉ *Grolmannstraße 32–33, 10623 Berlin-Charlottenburg,*
☎ *8803 2960,*
📠 *8803 29631.*

Pension Viola Nova (Map D–A4)
Excellent value for money; some of the larger rooms have several beds.
✉ *Kantstraße 146, 10623 Berlin-Charlottenburg,* ☎ *315 7260,* 📠 *312 3314.*

Below: *The Radisson SAS commands an excellent view of the Cathedral across the River Spree.*

Snacking Out
Germans are big **pork** eaters and renowned for their varieties of **sausage** – try any *Imbiss* fast-food stand in the street for a *Bockwurst* (boiled sausage), *Bratwurst* (grilled sausage) or the Berlin speciality *Currywurst* (sausage with a rich curry sauce). Also popular are spicy **meatballs** called *Bouletten* and various types of **pizza** and **kebab**.

Below: *Hearty German fare washed down with a beer or two. Lunch is usually the main meal of the day and dishes are often rather heavy.*

EATING OUT
Where to Eat

The variety of Berlin's **restaurants** is legendary – from **café** or **bistro** simplicity to palatial opulence, from traditional 1920s style to ultra-modern. Hundreds of restaurants serve the hearty fare for which Germany is famous; alongside them are French, Italian, Spanish, Turkish, Asian, Caribbean, Mexican and a host of **other nationalities**.

The latest fashionable area for dining out in Berlin is **Prenzlauer Berg**, the former working-class district just outside the centre, where countless restaurants and bars have opened in recent years. In **Kreuzberg**, too, there is plenty of scope to eat well and cheaply close to the city centre, while **Schöneberg** is also making its mark on the restaurant scene. By far the widest choice of places to eat is to be found in **Charlottenburg**, west of the Tiergarten between the radiating Ku'damm and Kantstraße. In the eastern section of the city, character restaurants have been incorporated into the restored **Nikolaiviertel**, while just north of the city centre **Oranienburger Straße** is the new place to head for.

What To Eat

The German capital is a veritable paradise for gourmets and snackers alike, with a profusion of restaurants, cafés, fast-food outlets and *Imbiss* street stalls. Since Germany's reunification in 1990, the eastern part of the city centre has spawned numerous new eating places, particularly in **Oranienburger Straße** and **Prenzlauer Berg** – both are worthy alternatives to the much-favoured **Ku'damm** area of Charlottenburg.

Above: *Berlin's café life still flourishes.*

Breakfast in Berlin can be either the full hotel works or it can be a café blow-out – whichever option you choose, you will probably eat enough to last you for most of the day. Some Berlin cafés serve 'breakfast' until early afternoon; at some cafés and notably on Sundays you can choose from at least half a dozen types of breakfast.

Lunch tends to be cheaper than **dinner**; for most Germans it is the main meal of the day. Both meals often start with **soup** – *Bohnensuppe* (bean soup), the Bavarian *Leberknödelsuppe* (a clear soup with liver-filled dumplings) and *Soljanke* (a spiced-up Ukranian soup) are favourites. Main courses are traditionally heavy, with **pork** a popular base: *Kassler Rippen* (smoked pork chops) and *Eisbein* (boiled pig's knuckle, usually served with pickled cabbage called *Sauerkraut*) are authentic Berlin dishes. Other pork-based dishes include all kinds of *Schnitzel*, *Schweinehaxe* (grilled pork knuckle) and *Schweinebraten* (roast pork), while **beef** and **chicken** are also available.

Big Breakfasts
Berlin is known for its all-day breakfast culture and the districts of Kreuzberg, Prenzlauer Berg and Friedrichshain offer buffets with style. Expect to pay between 5 and 9 euro for whatever you can eat. Two venues in Kreuzberg worth a look are:

Ankerklause
✉ Maybachufer 1
☎ 693 5649
Serves a wonderful Mexican breakfast.

Kuchen Kaiser
✉ Oranienplatz 11-13
☎ 614 02 697
Has a novel way of kiddie pricing, charging 50 cents per year of their age.

Freshwater **fish** include *Zander* (pike-perch), *Aal* (eel) and *Forelle* (trout). **Vegetables** generally focus on potatoes – fried as in *Bratkartoffeln*, mashed, jacket or boiled – and cabbage, often red and mixed with apple. Vegetarians, starved of decent vegetarian restaurants, could do worse than simply order a mixed salad; German **salads** are substantial and come served in their own dish. If you can find room, a typical German **dessert** is *Kompott* (stewed fruit).

Wine and Beer

Germany produces a fine range of **wines** (*see* panel, this page), and restaurants will also list international labels, particularly from France, Italy and Spain. But the favourite alcoholic drink by far is **beer** – Germans down 140 litres (246 pints) per head each year and the choice is enormous. As well as the ubiquitous draught Pils, there is bottled light beer, dark beer, wheat beer, old beer and even fruit beer; *Berliner Weisse* (Berlin White) is a frothy wheat beer served in a large bowl-shaped glass and mixed with raspberry or green woodruff syrup. Look out for *Weizenbier* (wheat beer) in *Hefe* (yeasty) and *Kristall* (clear) varieties. *Schwartzbier* is very dark beer, darker than *Dunkelbier*. *Bock* is a strong seasonal brew. Knock back a glass or two in a Berlin beer garden, an institution fit for a summer's day – there are excellent beer gardens in the suburbs, notably in Zehlendorf (west) and Köpenick (east). A winter tradition is to chase down the beer with a glass of Schnaps, a potent and warming distilled mix of alcohol and potato or fruits – mainly apricots, plums or cherries.

German Wine

Forget the ubiquitous **Liebfraumilch**: the majority of Berlin restaurants can offer a selection of quality German wines that will not have you clamouring for French or Italian. Most German wine is **white**, owing to a shortage of grape-ripening sunshine in northern latitudes, but a limited amount of **Rhine red** is produced. The **Rhine** and **Mosel** valleys are the chief producing areas, with the **Main River** in **Franconia** and **Baden** also contributing. Cheaper wines are classified as *Tafelwein* (table wine); popular varieties unclude Riesling, Traminer, Niersteiner Domtal, Piesporter and Oppenheimer. Note that Rhine wine comes in brown rather than green bottles.

Eastern City

• LUXURY

Französischer Hof

Art Nouveau splendour on the Gendarmenmarkt; the cuisine is German-French.

✉ Jägerstraße 56, Mitte, ☎ 204 3570.

Kaiserstuben

Quiet room in a former 18th-century palace. Imaginative menu with four-course meal for 49 euro. Afterwards, enjoy tea from a samovar in the Tadjikistan Room.

✉ Am Festungsgraben 1, Mitte, ☎ 2061 0548.

Vau

Leading chef Kolja Kleeberg has further established what has become one of Berlin's leading gourmet addresses.

✉ Jägerstraße 54–55, Mitte, ☎ 202 9730.

Zur Gerichtslaube

Enjoy typical Berlin fare beneath the vaulted ceiling of the Nikolaiviertel's rebuilt former courthouse, dating from 1270.

✉ Poststraße 28, Mitte, ☎ 241 5697.

• MID-RANGE

Borchardt

The place to dine after the show: this restaurant offers late-evening dining for theatre-goers.

✉ Französische Straße 47, Mitte, ☎ 2038 7110.

Café Oren

Top Jewish and Arab fare served in this café close to the New Synagogue.

✉ Oranienburger Straße 28, Mitte, ☎ 282 8228.

Fernsehturm Telecafé

The restaurant in the TV tower, 207m (680ft) above Berlin, offers great views and an excellent meal selection.

✉ Panoramastraße 1A, Mitte, ☎ 242 3333.

Lutter & Wegner

Austrian-style restaurant offering outstanding game dishes. The Weinstube serves meat and cheese dishes until late.

✉ Charlottenstraße 56, Mitte, ☎ 2029 5417.

Opernpalais

Here you can choose from the Operncafé (patisserie), Königin Luise (gourmet) and Operntreff, a Parisian-style café.

✉ Unter den Linden 5, Mitte, ☎ 202 683.

Reinhard's

Effectively recreates the refined atmosphere of 1920s Berlin in the old Nikolaiviertel.

✉ Poststraße 28, Mitte, ☎ 242 5295.

Sophieneck

Good home cooking in a cosy atmosphere.

✉ Grosse Hamburger Straße 37, Mitte, ☎ 238 4065.

Zum Nussbaum

A recreated 16th-century Nikolaiviertel restaurant bombed out of existence in World War II. Touristy but deservedly popular.

✉ Am Nussbaum 3, Mitte, ☎ 242 3095.

Zur Letzen Instanz

Artists and celebrities frequent Berlin's oldest restaurant in a pub just south of Alexanderplatz.
⊠ Waisenstraße 14-16, Mitte, ☎ 242 5528.

• BUDGET
Café Adler

Next to the former Checkpoint Charlie, it was the last building in West Berlin in its former life as a pharmacy.
⊠ Friedrichstraße 206, Kreuzberg, ☎ 251 8965.

Monsieur Vuong

This is a good-value eatery serving Vietnamese cuisine. Limited menu changes every two days; reservations are not accepted.
⊠ Alte Schönhauser Straße 46, Mitte, ☎ 3087 2643.

Trefpunkt Berlin

The name means 'meeting point' – an inexpensive eatery with bags of character in the Friedrichstraße district. Berlin specialities to the fore.
⊠ Mittelstraße 55, Mitte, ☎ 204 1819.

Weihenstephaner

Well-priced Bavarian fare can be found in this venue by Hackescher Markt station. The beer is from Weihenstephaner, Germany's oldest brewery.
⊠ Neue Promenade 5, Mitte, ☎ 2576 2871.

Zur Nolle

Comfortable 1920s-style restaurant in one of the 13 converted railway arches by Friedrichstraße station.
⊠ Bahnhof Friedrichstraße, Mitte, ☎ 208 2655.

Western City
• LUXURY
Alt Luxemburg

Enjoy cuisine with a French accent in the refined atmosphere of one of Berlin's top restaurants.
⊠ Windscheidstraße 31, Charlottenburg, ☎ 323 8730.

Ana E Bruno

Classic Italian restaurant named after its owners, known for its four- and eight-course meals. Warm and informal atmosphere.
⊠ Sophie-Charlotten-Straße 101, Charlottenburg, ☎ 325 7110.

Bamberger Reiter

Reservations are advised for this farmhouse-style venue with one of Berlin's top reputations.
⊠ Regensburger Straße 7, Schöneberg, ☎ 218 4282.

Dachgarten Restaurant Käfer am Bundestag

Dine at the top of the Reichstag building looking out on to Sir Norman Foster's dome. Reservation advised.
⊠ The Reichstag, Platz der Republik, Tiergarten, ☎ 2262 9933.

Ponte Vecchio

Fine Tuscan specialities in relaxing and unpretentious sur-

roundings, well worth its Michelin star.
✉ *Spielhagenstraße 3, Charlottenburg,* ☎ *342 1999.*

Spree-Athen

One of Berlin's best-known restaurants, it recaptures the spirit of imperial Berlin, with songs to match.
✉ *Leibnitzstraße 60, Charlottenburg,* ☎ *324 1733.*

• *MID-RANGE*
Arche Noah

Widely acclaimed kosher restaurant in the Jüdisches Gemeindehaus (Jewish Community Centre).
✉ *Fasanenstraße 79–80, Charlottenburg,* ☎ *882 6138.*

Café Kranzler

Berlin's best-known coffee and cake house, it was formerly situated on Unter den Linden. A tourist hot spot, but the balcony is good people-watching territory.
✉ *Kurfürstendamm 18, Charlottenburg,* ☎ *887 183 925.*

Cassambalis

Mediterranean-style restaurant with a wide menu and a delightfully relaxed atmosphere – a far cry from its early incarnation as boisterous Hecker's Deele.
✉ *Grolmanstraße 35, Charlottenburg,* ☎ *885 4747.*

Cour Carree

Tempting fish selection on an imaginative French menu. Dine on the leafy terrace looking on to the fashionable Berlin square.
✉ *Savignyplatz 5, Charlottenburg,* ☎ *312 5238.*

Der Ägypter

Dine authentic Egyptian without having to cross the Mediterranean: lots of lamb and felafel and a great vegetarian selection, all beneath a back-lit mask of the boy king Tutankhamun.
✉ *Kantstraße 26, Charlottenburg,* ☎ *313 9230.*

Café Culture

The café culture is alive and well in Berlin, from Charlottenburg in the west to Friedrichshain in the east. Two to try in **Charlottenburg** are **Leysieffer**, ✉ Kurfürstendamm 218, ☎ 885 7480, where the cakes are among the best in the city, and the **Café in Literaturhaus**, ✉ Fasanenstraße 23, ☎ 882 5414, a venue for writers and critics next to a bookstore.

In **Mitte**, **Assel**, ✉ Oranienburgerstraße 21, ☎ 281 2056, has a bohemian feel to it, while **Kurhaus**, ✉ Alte Schönhauser Straße 35, offers healthy fruit and vegetable juices in a café that's also a shirt shop.

In **Prenzlauer Berg**, go for **Al Hamra**, ✉ Raumerstraße 16, ☎ 4285 0095; in **Kreuzberg** make for **Café am Engelbecken**, ✉ Heinrich Heine Platz.

Engelbecken

Quality Bavarian and Alpine fare. Reserve a terrace table at one of Berlin's best open-air dining locations. ✉ Witzlebenstraße 31, Charlottenburg, ☎ 615 2810.

Florian

Popular with the literati for its Bavarian cuisine. ✉ Grolmannstraße 52, Charlottenburg, ☎ 313 9184.

Marjellchen

A real rarity, serving fare from East Prussia, Pomerania and Silesia. There's a nice bar too. ✉ Mommsenstraße 9, Charlottenburg, ☎ 883 2676.

Sachiko Sushi

Berlin's first conveyor-belt sushi restaurant, it continues to be as popular as ever. ✉ Grolmannstraße 47, Charlottenburg, ☎ 313 2282.

Storch

Berlin's leading Alsatian restaurant, Storch is just a few minutes' walk from Schöneberg Town Hall. ✉ Wartburgstraße 54, Schöneberg, ☎ 784 2059.

Woolloomooloo

Named after a Sydney neighbourhood, it serves Aussie fare that's some of the best in the Northern Hemisphere. ✉ Röntgenstraße 7, Charlottenburg, ☎ 3470 2777.

• BUDGET
Luisen-Bräu

A cheap and highly cheerful restaurant – where you can have good plain food washed down with home-brewed beer. It is located near Schloß Charlottenburg. ✉ Luisenplatz 1, Charlottenburg, ☎ 341 9388

Prenzlauer Berg
Gugelhof

Alsatian restaurant among the first in the Kollwitzplatz area in the mid-1990s.

Excellent charcuterie and a good wine list.
✉ *Stubbenkammerstraße 8,* ☎ *445 8502.*

Istoria

Authentic Greek fare, ranging from commonplace to creative, is served in this restaurant situated just off Kollwitzplatz.
✉ *Kollwitzstraße 64,* ☎ *4405 0208.*

La Focacceria

Good for classic Italian dishes and some of the best pizzas in town. The crust doesn't come much thinner.
✉ *Fehrbelliner Straße 24,* ☎ *4403 2771.*

Lappeggi

Named after a brothel owner, this spacious but relaxing trattoria covers the Italian range, from simple pasta upwards.
✉ *Kollwitzstraße 56,* ☎ *442 6347.*

Pasternak

Well-rated Russian speciality restaurant.
✉ *Knaackstraße 22–24,* ☎ *441 3399.*

Restauration 1900

Acclaimed bistro-style eating and drinking house on the north side of Kollwitzplatz.
✉ *Husemannstraße 1,* ☎ *442 2494.*

Salsabil

Inexpensive Arabic restaurant; private alcoves, low tables.
✉ *Raumerstraße 14,* ☎ *4403 3846.*

Kreuzberg
Abendmahl

Booking is recommended for Berlin's top-ranked vegetarian restaurant. There is also fish on the menu and the soups are excellent.
✉ *Muskauer Straße 9, Kreuzberg,* ☎ *612 5170.*

Altes Zollhaus

Restored customs house by the Landwehrkanal in north Kreuzberg serving mid-priced German fare. Attractive summer garden.
✉ *Carl-Herz-Ufer 30, Kreuzberg,* ☎ *692 3300.*

Dark Dining
To experience the dark side of Berlin's cuisine, head for **Nocti Vagus – The Dark Restaurant** in Prenzlauer Berg. Here you dine in total darkness – a new experience designed to appeal to all the senses. Serving in the restaurant are blind or visually impaired waiters who have undergone special training. The menu changes every day and includes meat, fish, poultry and vegetarian dishes.
✉ Saarbrücker Straße 36-38, in an old industrial building called the Backfabrik ☎ 7474 9123 ◷ from 18:00

Get on the Net
Internet cafés have sprung up all over Berlin in recent years and you won't need to leg it far to log on. In Charlottenburg there's the **Internet-Terminal**, ✉ Kantstraße 38; in Mitte you'll find **Netlounge**, ✉ Auguststraße 89. Trendy Prenzlauer Berg is well equipped for surfers – **Alpha Internet-Café** is at ✉ Dunckerstraße 72 and you'll find **Internetwork Berlin** at ✉ Gaudystraße 1.

Above: *The Kaiser-Wilhelm-Gedacht-niskirche overlooks a street café.*

Paris Bar

If you are dead set on rubbing shoulders with celebrities, there's just one place to go in Berlin – the Paris Bar. Simply elegant, it has hosted big names from Madonna to Mikhail Gorbachev; many diners come before or after a performance at the nearby Theater des Westens. Paris Bar is at ✉ Kantstraße 152, ☎ 313 8052.

Austria

Enjoy Viennese coffee specialities and wholesome Austrian cooking in rustic surroundings.

✉ *Bergmannstraße 30, Kreuzberg,*
☎ *694 4440.*

Hostaria del Monte Croce

Good Italian eatery in west Kreuzberg. The restaurant has its own courtyard.

✉ *Mittenwalderstraße 6, Kreuzberg,*
☎ *694 3968.*

Siralti

Enjoy classic Turkish cuisine in the south of Berlin's Turkish quarter.

✉ *Schleiermacher-straße 14, Kreuzberg,*
☎ *6904 1380.*

Terra Anatolia

Excellent Turkish cooking – specialities include dishes baked in a special Anatolian oven.

✉ *Hauptstraße 65, Schöneberg,*
☎ *859 4801.*

Friedrichs-hain

Aotearoa

This restaurant's name means 'Land of the Long White Cloud', the Maori name for New Zealand. Lamb dishes, not surprisingly, are prominent on the menu.

✉ *Weichselstraße 26A,* ☎ *2977 0582.*

Noi Quattro

Highly rated Italian restaurant with plenty of flair in the cooking.

✉ *Strausberger Platz 2,* ☎ *2404 5622.*

ENTERTAINMENT
Cinema

The spirit of prewar Berlin is recaptured in *Berlin Wie es War* (Berlin As It Was) at the **Adria Filmtheater** in the southern district of Steglitz. At the start of the 1940s, before Berlin had been subjected to the devastating wartime Allied bombing, film-maker Leo de Laforgue filmed life in the city with a simple hand-held camera; banned by Goebbels in 1942, the film finally reached the screen in 1950. Also showing is a film on the Royal Palace demolished in 1950.

Above: Bertolt Brecht statue near the Berliner Ensemble theatre.

Theatre

Berlin's theatre scene comes in two halves – it is split between the west and east of the city centre. Venues in the western part are centred around the Ku'damm; in the eastern part they are spread out north and west of Friedrichstraße Station. The most interesting venues are in the east – for instance the **Berliner Ensemble**, concentrating on Bertolt Brecht and Shakespeare classics, and the **Deutsches Theater** (*see* page 72), known for the quality of its productions both classic and modern. Another eastern venue of note is the **Maxim Gorki Theater**, which focuses mainly on Russian works, but also produces works by a variety of European playwrights.

Variety and musical performances first appeared on Berlin's theatre scene more than 100 years ago, and today venues such as the **Wintergarten** are keeping alive the arts of juggling, magic and acrobatics. The **Friedrichstadtpalast**, meanwhile, is Europe's largest revue theatre with a reputation to match. There is a touch of Broadway glamour at the **Theater des Westens**, which

---

Adria Filmtheater
✉ Schloßstraße 48, Steglitz
☎ 0180 5050 711 (0.12 euro/minute)
🕐 *Berlin Wie es War* shows Sun at 11:30

Berliner Ensemble
✉ Bertolt-Brecht-Platz 1, Mitte
☎ 284 080
💻 www.berliner-ensemble.de

Maxim Gorki Theater
✉ Am Festungsgraben 2, Mitte
☎ 2022 1115
💻 www.gorki.de

Wintergarten Varieté
✉ Potsdamer Straße 96, Tiergarten
☎ 2500 8888
💻 www.wintergarten-variete.de

Friedrichstadtpalast
✉ Friedrichstraße 107, Mitte
☎ 2326 2326
💻 www.friedrichstadtpalast.de

Above: *The Deutsches Theater, where Marlene Dietrich made her stage debut.*

steers clear of international hit shows of the type staged by the **Schiller-Theater** and instead stages classics and home-produced musicals – imagination and creative flair are the bywords here.

Deutsches Theater

The Deutsches Theater on Schumannstraße was founded in 1883 and prospered under the direction of Otto Brahm and under impressario Max Reinhardt; busts of both men line the theatre's forecourt. This was where **Marlene Dietrich** made her stage debut in 1922; after many appearances in silent films, her seductive role eight years later in *Der Blaue Engel* (The Blue Angel) elevated her to stardom.

Berlin Concert Hall

The **Konzerthaus Berlin** was designed by Karl Friedrich Schinkel and seats 1850 patrons. It is currently home to the **Berlin Symphony Orchestra**. In front is a splendid white marble statue of the great German dramatist and romantic poet Friedrich Schiller by Reinhold Begas.

Street Parties
Carnival has never really found its way to Berlin and the traditional carnival day (Rosenmontag, the Monday before Lent) is a normal working day in the capital. But Berlin nevertheless sports some lively summer street happenings. Look out for news of the **Love Parade**, the colourful **Carnival of Cultures**, the gay community's **Christopher Street Day Parade** and the **Fête de la Musique**.

Theatreland

Berlin's theatreland is located immediately to the north of Friedrichstraße station. Across Friedrichstraße from the Tränenpalast is the contrasting **Admiralspalast** with its fine fluted columns and bas-reliefs. It was built in 1910 and now houses two theatres – the satirical cabaret **Die Distel** and, across an attractive inner courtyard, the restored **Metropol** (*see* below) given to staging lighter musical productions. On the opposite side of the River Spree and across a small park on Bertold-Brecht-Platz is the **Berliner Ensemble** theatre, with a rather austere exterior that does very little to enhance its run-down surroundings. Bertolt Brecht founded the theatre after his return from American exile; performances of the great man's work are staged regularly. In the park are a seated statue of Brecht and three marble pillars bearing his words.

Metropol

Nollendorfplatz was a hub of Berlin nightlife and the centre of the city's gay community in the 1920s and 1930s. The Metropol now hosts events for the gay community and is a popular venue for fans of **pop**, **rock**, **Indie** and **punk** music.

Cabaret

Berlin's reputation for all-singing, all-dancing cabaret is legion, though nowadays the performances are more akin to variety shows aimed at international consumption. Visitors should take care not to confuse cabaret with Kabarett, the acerbic political satires for which rather more than a working knowledge of German is needed.

Theater des Westens
✉ Kantstraße 12, Charlottenburg
☎ 0180 599 8999
🖥 www.theater-des-westens.de

Schiller-Theater
✉ Bismarckstraße 110, Charlottenburg
☎ 847 200 312

Deutsches Theater
✉ Schumannstraße 13A, Mitte
☎ 284 410
🖥 www.deutsches-theater.berlin.net

Berlin Concert Hall
✉ Gendarmenmarkt 2, Mitte
☎ 203 090
🖥 www.konzerthaus.de

Metropol
✉ Nollendorfplatz 5, Schöneberg
☎ 216 4122

Right: *Music in Berlin takes many forms – from classical concerts to impromptu pavement performances.*

Rock the Joint
Berlin's rock music scene is alive and kicking, with countless venues to keep aficionados happy. The **KulturBrauerei**, ✉ Schönhauser Allee 35, Prenzlauer Berg, ☎ 443 1515, is a former brewery with a variety of venues. As well as NBI (*see* listing, page 75), the three main venues are Kesselhaus, Palas and Maschinehaus.
Columbiahalle, ✉ Columbiadamm 13-21, ☎ 6110 1313, in the southern district of Tempelhof, is a spacious venue regularly hosting big names and top hip-hop performers. In Kreuzberg, look for **Festsaal Kreuzberg**, ✉ Skalitzer Straße 130, ☎ 6165 6003 – it's strong on Indie with ace DJs appearing. **Arena Berlin**, ✉ Eichenstraße 4, Treptow, is a one-time bus garage staging top-line concerts.

Nightlife

Berlin's night scene is an ever-changing collection of discos, music bars and the like. What is there one year may have gone the next; *see* page 75 for a few of the ever-presents.

If a beer beckons you after a long day's museum bashing, look for a sign saying 'Kneipe' – it means 'pub'. There are hundreds, if not thousands, in Berlin, so it won't take you too long to find one. Many Berlin bars also serve light meals and most keep extremely sociable hours – closing time is generally reckoned to be any time between midnight and 04:00.

Bars and Pubs

Bar am Lützowplatz

This is a large, traditional cocktail bar that claims to be among the best in the world.

✉ Lützowplatz, Schöneberg,
☎ 262 6807.

Broker's Bier Börse

Customers determine the prices for 16 draught beers in this stock exchange theme pub – the greater the demand, the higher the price (and vice versa). Good food is available too.

✉ Schiffbauerdamm 8, Mitte, ☎ 872 293.

CSA Bar

There's a retro Soviet feel to this hangout, named after the Czech Republic airline that used to be housed here.

✉ Karl-Marx-Allee 96, Friedrichshain,
☎ 2904 4741.

Felsenkeller

This is an established bar which now attracts a much younger clientele.

✉ Akazienstraße 2, Schöneberg,
☎ 781 3447.

Green Door

Elite cocktail bar where you have to ring the bell to get in, in the style of an exclusive club.

✉ Winterfeldstraße 50, Tiergarten,
☎ 215 2515.

Leydicke

Old-style drinking establishment worth visiting for the traditional ambience alone. It has been run by the same family for over a century.

✉ Mansteinstraße 4, Schöneberg,
☎ 216 2973.

Mutter Hoppe

Old-fashioned Berlin pub serving good hearty food. Songs from the 1920s and 1930s on Friday and Saturday evenings.

✉ Rathausstraße 21, Mitte,
☎ 241 5625.

Robbengatter

Pool bar offering good food and drink.

✉ Grunewaldstraße 55, Schöneberg,
☎ 853 5255.

Bars with Music

Bar Lounge 808

Gilt columns and heavy drapes characterize this Mitte venue, strong on house music with comfy sofas to chill out on.

✉ Oranienburger Straße 42, Mitte,
☎ 2804 6727.

Irish Harp Pub

This pub is full of traditional Irish cheer, often with live music. (More Guinness at the Irish Bar in the Europa-Center and Quinns at Schönhauser Allee 6–7.)

✉ Giesebrechtstraße 15, Charlottenburg,
☎ 882 7739.

NBI

Leading location for electronic music, NBI (the letters stand for 'New Berlin Initiative')

Cocktail Time

The cocktail boom in Berlin has led to a mushrooming of lounge-style bars – nowhere better illustrated than in the former run-down East Berlin district of Friedrichshain. Around the U-Bahn/S-Bahn station of Warschauer Straße, popular venues include **Dachkammer**, ✉ Simon-Dach-Straße 39, ☎ 296 1673 – two bars in one – and the **Astro Bar**, ✉ Simon-Dach-Straße 40, with its 1960s flashback style. There's also **Die Tagung**, strong on Ostalgie with memorabilia of the old GDR, ✉ Wühlisch-straße 29, ☎ 292 8756, and **Stereo 33**, ✉ Krossener Straße 24, ☎ 9599 9433 – a supercool venue in minimalist design. **Habana**, ✉ Grünberger Straße 57, ☎ 2694 8661, offers a Cuban-style Latin flavour with a touch of class.

now has a new home in the KulturBrauerei entertainment complex.
✉ Schönhauser Allee 36, Prenzlauer Berg, ☎ 4405 1681.

Cabaret

Bar jeder Vernunft

Adventurous theatre a few blocks south of the zoo; be prepared for the unexpected.
✉ Schaperstraße 24, Wilmersdorf, ☎ 883 1582.

Chamäleon Varieté

Traditional variety in the restored Hackesche Höfe: clowns, jugglers, acrobats and the like.
✉ Rosenthaler Straße 40–41 (Hackesche Höfe), Mitte, ☎ 400 0590.

Chez Nous

Berlin folk are fond of their transvestite shows – this one is especially popular and therefore reservations are advised.
✉ Marburger Straße 14, Charlottenburg, ☎ 213 1810.

Friedrichstadt-palast

Europe's biggest revue theatre and the eastern city's best-known night spot. It is very popular with tour groups – book early.
✉ Friedrichstraße 107, Mitte, ☎ 2326 2326.

Scheinbar Varieté

Twenties-style revues in Berlin's southern suburb.
✉ Monumenten-straße 9, Schöneberg, ☎ 784 5539.

Tränenpalast

It's now a theatre, but was once the building through which Western visitors departed the East in the divided city.
✉ Reichstagufer 17, Mitte, ☎ 2061 0011.

Wintergarten Varieté

Top-quality entertainers make it a night out to remem-

ber – this venue offers a great mix of cabaret and variety. Dine before the show.
✉ Potsdamer Straße 96, Tiergarten, ☎ 250 0880.

Nightclubs
Big Eden
Rolf Eden's nightclubs were a focal part of the pre-Wende West Berlin night scene and remain so today.
✉ Kurfürstendamm 202, Charlottenburg, ☎ 882 6120.

Far Out
One of the classic Berlin discos – the place for dance fans to be.
✉ Kurfürstendamm 156, Charlottenburg, ☎ 3200 0724.

90 Grad
Classic club venue for disco, acid jazz, hip-hop and funk.
✉ Dennewitzstraße 37, Mitte, ☎ 2759 6231.

Oxymoron
This popular nightspot in Hof 1 recaptures 1920s flair with its stylish bar.
✉ Rosenthaler Straße 40–41 (Hackescher Höfe), Mitte, ☎ 2839 1886.

Quasimodo
Long-established venue for live jazz, funk, blues and soul. It is usually packed; there is no charge on Tue and Wed.
✉ Kantstraße 12a, Charlottenburg, ☎ 312 8086.

Gambling
If you've cash to spare after a long round of clubbing and nightlife, hit the casinos. **Casino Berlin** is on the 37th floor of the Park Inn Hotel, ✉ Alexanderplatz, ☎ 2389 4144, while **Spielbank Berlin**, ✉ Marlene-Dietrich-Platz 1 in the new Potsdamer Platz development, ☎ 255 990, has three floors of gaming and claims to be Germany's largest casino.

Below: *Berlin's broad nightclub scene provides after-dark activities for every taste.*

Above: *Visit Potsdam for its parks and palaces, but don't overlook its pleasant traffic-free Old Town.*

BBS Berliner Bären Stadtrundfahrt
✉ Seeburger Straße 19b, 13581 Berlin-Spandau
☎ 3519 5270

Berolina
✉ Meinekestraße 3, 10719 Berlin-Charlottenburg
☎ 8856 8030

BVB Bus-Verkehr-Berlin
✉ Grenzallee 15, 12057 Berlin
☎ 683 8910

Severin + Kühn
✉ Kurfürstendamm 216, 10719 Berlin-Charlottenburg
☎ 880 4190

EXCURSIONS

Berlin's rather wide streets make the city ideal for sightseeing from the comfort of a twin-deck **excursion bus**, and full-day and half-day tours operate daily. The classic hop-on, hop-off City-Circle sightseeing tour with commentary in eight languages operates from April to October with **Berolina**, **BBS**, **BVB** and **Severin + Kühn**. The complete trip takes two hours, but half-hourly departures allow you to jump off and reboard at 15 stops around the city; your ticket is valid for a day. A similar Top-Tour-Berlin offer from the local transport authority BVG makes 20 stops along the way and includes Schloß Charlottenburg.

Cheaper by far is the 100 regular **bus** service, which runs from the Zoo station right through the middle of Berlin to Prenzlauer Berg. A standard single ticket allows you two hours to get off as many times as you like while heading in the same direction. Full-day trips operate to Dresden and Meissen, and also to Spreewald, including a punting trip. There are half-day excursions to Potsdam/Sanssouci and trips out to the Berlin lakes.

For many, however, the best way to see Berlin is **on foot**, and Berlin Walks has three walking tours of the city. You do not need to pre-book – all you have to do is turn up at the meeting point by the Zoo station. More information is available from the tourist office (*see page 84*).

A number of companies operate **boat trips** in and around Berlin – there are trips on the Spree and the Landwehrkanal, and you can also go further afield between Spandau, Wannsee and Potsdam.

POTSDAM

For almost three decades, the Wall separated western Berlin from its immediate and older neighbour. The Brandenburg capital is only 24km (15 miles) from central Berlin and with excellent rail connections (S-Bahn to Potsdam Hauptbahnhof), it makes a thoroughly worthwhile day trip – or even an extension of two or three days. The chief attraction, **Sanssouci Park** with its palaces and pavilions, lies immediately west of the Old Town; some 3km (2 miles) northeast is the **Schloß Cecilienhof**, scene of the 1945 Potsdam Conference.

Altstadt

Though the palaces and parks provide the chief reason for a visit to Potsdam, do not overlook the Altstadt (Old Town), with its superb collection of 18th-century buildings. Pedestrianized **Brandenburger Straße**, Potsdam's principal shopping street, connects the Luisenplatz at its western end with the Bassinplatz, where a couple of historical churches are located – the **Französische Kirche** (French Church), built for the Huguenot community in 1753, and also the **Peter-Pauls-Kirche** from 1868. South of Bassinplatz, the **Holländisches Viertel** (Dutch Quarter) contains many 18th-century red-brick gabled houses built for Dutch immigrant workers, some of which have been restored. On Am Alten Markt are the lovely domed **Nikolai-**

Potsdam
Location: Map A
Distance from Berlin: 24km (15 miles)

Reederei Bruno Winkler
✉ Mierendorffstraße 16, 10589 Berlin-Charlottenburg
☎ 349 9595

Stern und Kreis
✉ Puschkinallee 15, 12435 Berlin-Treptow
☎ 536 3600

Tempelhofer Reisen
✉ Werkring 5-7, 13597 Berlin-Spandau
☎ 752 3061

Top-Tour-Berlin
✉ BVG Stadttouristik, Helmholzstraße 41, 10587 Berlin-Charlottenburg
☎ 2562 4740

Below: *These 18th-century gabled houses are in the Dutch quarter of Potsdam.*

Filmmuseum Potsdam
✉ Marstall am Lust-garten, Breite Straße 1A, 14467 Potsdam
☎ 0331 271 810
🕓 daily 10:00–18:00

Sanssouci Park
✉ Maulbeerallee, 14471 Potsdam
☎ 0331 969 4190
🕓 palace Tue–Sun 09:00–17:00 Apr–Oct, 09:00–16:00 Nov–Mar; park 09:00 to dusk daily

kirche (St Nicholas Church), built to Schinkel's neo-Classical plans in 1850, and the **Altes Rathaus** (Old Town Hall) from 1753, now containing art galleries and a cellar restaurant. Another old building put to good use is Knobelsdorff's elegant **Marstall**, the former royal stables from the 1740s that now house the **Filmmuseum**, with material obtained from the nearby Babelsberg Film Studios.

Sanssouci Park

The Schloß Sanssouci has pride of place in the massive Sanssouci Park, which covers some 300ha (741 acres) and stretches a good 2km (1 mile) from the centre of Potsdam. The park's splendid array of other buildings includes the **Bildergalerie** (Picture Gallery), purpose-built in 1764 and containing works of masters such as Rubens, Caravaggio and Van Dyck; it is situated just east of the palace. On the western side is the **Neue Kammern** (New Chambers), now used as a guesthouse; about 500m (550yd) southwest of the palace is the delightful **Chinesisches Teehaus** (Chinese Tea House), from 1757, its circular roof supported by gilded palm trees and bearing a gilded Mandarin. West of the palace are the **Orangerie**, a Renaissance-style building of 1864 that accommodated visiting royalty, and also the **Sizilianischer Garten** (Sicilian Garden), complete with subtropical plants. In the south of the park is the **Schloß Charlottenhof**, built in 1826 by Karl Friedrich Schinkel. The park is a legacy of King Frederick the Great who built terraced gardens before adding the showpiece palace.

Below: *Schloß Sanssouci is Potsdam's showpiece, a summer retreat for Frederick the Great.*

LEIPZIG

Leipzig's origins go back 1000 years, but the city's name is firmly etched on recent history as the focus of peaceful protest by tens of thousands of GDR citizens that was seen as a prelude to the toppling of the Wall. The citizens of Leipzig, 181km (113 miles) south of Berlin, played a leading role in the **democratic revolution** of 1989 and, in October of that year, they organized demonstration marches against the GDR's dictatorship. A mass rally on 9 October was followed a week later by an estimated 120,000 taking to Leipzig's streets in a demonstration the like of which had not been seen before. The GDR government capitulated and within a month the Wall had collapsed. The elections that followed led to the reunification of Germany.

Most of Leipzig's historic buildings are clustered in the **Altstadt**, within the ring road that follows the line of the old city wall. At its heart is the cobbled **Marktplatz**, with the magnificent Renaissance **Altes Rathaus** (Old Town Hall) of 1556 taking up the whole of the square's eastern side; there are shops at ground floor level and the **Leipzig History Museum** on the first floor.

Behind the town hall is the **Alte Börse** (Old Exchange) of 1687, now a cultural centre with a monument to Goethe, who studied law at nearby **Leipzig University**. The University fronts Augustusplatz, the focus of the city's cultural and academic life; on the square's northern side is the **Opera House**, a neo-Classical creation of the communists from 1960, and on its southern edge the **Neues Gewandhaus**, the city's major concert and jazz venue.

Leipzig
Location: Map C–B3
Distance from Berlin: 181km (113 miles)
Fast Inter-City Express (ICE) trains link Berlin (Hauptbahnhof) and Leipzig; the journey takes one hour and 15 minutes.

Leipzig Tourist Service
⊠ Richard-Wagner-Straße 1, 04109 Leipzig
☎ 0341 710 4260
🖳 www.leipzig.de
🕘 Mon–Fri 10:00–18:00, Sat–Sun 09:00–16:00, holidays 10:00–16:00

Opera House
⊠ Augustusplatz 12, 04109 Leipzig
☎ 0341 126 1261
🕘 box office Mon–Fri 10:00–20:00, Sat 10:00–16:00

Leipzig History Museum
⊠ Altes Rathaus, Markt 1, 04109 Leipzig
☎ 0341 965 1320
🕘 Tue–Sun 10:00–18:00

Neues Gewandhaus
⊠ Augustusplatz 8, 04109 Leipzig
☎ 0341 127 0280
🕘 box office Mon–Fri 10:00–18:00, Sat 10:00–14:00

Dresden
Location: Map C–C3
Distance from Berlin:
195km (121 miles)
Inter-City trains link
Berlin (Hauptbahnhof)
and Dresden; the jour-
ney takes 2 hours and
15 minutes.

Dresden China
You can buy it in dedi-
cated Berlin shops on
the Ku'damm and along
Unter den Linden – the
attractive porcelain bearing the blue crossed-
swords trademark that
identifies it as Dresden
china. If you take an
excursion to Dresden
you can also visit the
factory in Talstraße,
Meissen (more fully the
Staatliche Porzellan-
Manufaktur Meissen).
Guided tours of the
workshops show the
complete production
process, but expect long
queues at this most pop-
ular attraction in sum-
mer. Displays in the
Schauhalle show the
changing porcelain styles
through the years.

DRESDEN

A two-hour Autobahn trip 195km (121 miles)
south of Berlin is Dresden, tagged 'the Flo-
rence of the North' centuries ago because of
its splendid **architecture**. Most of Dresden's
finest buildings date from the 17th century
and were captured on canvas by **Canaletto**,
court painter at the time of **August the
Strong** of Saxony (1670–1733). But on the
night of 13 February 1945, Dresden was
reduced to rubble and ashes as British and
American aircraft blitzed the city in one of
World War II's most destructive **bombing
raids** that cost some 50,000 lives; over half a
century on, the reconstruction continues.

First-time visitors should head for
Theaterplatz to see two of the city's finest
creations – the Zwinger (Festival Square) and
Semperoper (Semper Opera House), both
destroyed in the war and rebuilt in their
original style. The **Zwinger**, completed in
1710, is regarded as a Baroque masterpiece.
Note the **Glockenspielpavillon**, where a car-
illon of 40 Meissen porcelain bells hangs
either side of the blue clock. Museums and
galleries in the Zwinger include the **Old
Masters Gallery** and **Porcelain Collection**.

The original **Semperoper**, named after
Dresden's leading 19th-century architect

Gottfried Semper, dates
from 1841; the present
rebuild was completed in
1985. Close to the Albert-
inum, on Neumarkt is the
Frauenkirche (Church of
Our Lady), destroyed in
World War II but now
restored; it is Germany's
largest Protestant church.

Left: *The Semper-oper in Dresden, re-built after the war.*
Opposite: *The Zwinger in Dresden is classic Baroque.*

SPREEWALD

An hour by rail southeast of Berlin brings you to **Lübben** and **Lübbenau** in the very heart of the Spreewald (Spree Forest), a scenic area crisscrossed by 400km (250 miles) of rivers and canals where a boat or punt offers one of the best ways of getting around. The region is also great for **hiking** and **fishing**, and on warm summer weekends thousands of Berliners come in their droves to overdose on rest and relaxation. The self-styled 'capital' of the region is picturesque Lübbenau. (*See* Map C–C3.)

BUCKOW

The village of Buckow lies 50km (31 miles) east of Berlin, in a 200km² (77 sq mile) country park of meandering rivers, lakes and hills known as **Märkische Schweiz** (Switzerland of the March). It came to the attention of Berliners in the 1950s, when playwright **Bertolt Brecht** and actress **Helene Weigel** spent their summers away from the city in a house that has since been turned into a museum, the **Brecht-Weigel House**. The house, still with its original furnishings, is where Brecht wrote most of his *Buckow Elegies* in 1953. (*See* Map C–C2.)

Dresden-Werbung und Tourismus
✉ Ostra-Allee 11, 01067 Dresden
☎ 0351 4919 2100
🖥 www.dresden.de
Tourist information:
✉ P. Rager Straße 1
🕐 Apr–Oct Mon–Fri 09:30–18:30, Sat 09:30–18:00; Nov–Mar Mon–Fri 10:00–18:00, Sat 10:00–16:00

Old Masters Gallery
✉ Semper building, Zwinger, 01067 Dresden
☎ 0351 4914 2000
🕐 Tue–Sun 10:00–18:00

Porcelain Collection
✉ Glockenspielpavillon, Zwinger, 01067 Dresden
☎ 0351 4914 2000
🕐 Tue–Sun 10:00–18:00

Semperoper
✉ Theaterplatz 2, 01067 Dresden
☎ 0351 4911 705
🕐 for visits, Mon–Fri 10:00–18:00, Sat–Sun 10:00–13:00 or 16:00

Brecht-Weigel House
✉ Bertolt-Brecht-Straße 29, 15377 Buckow
☎ 033 433 467
🕐 Apr–Oct Wed–Fri 13:00–17:00, Sat–Sun 13:00–18:00; Nov–Mar Wed–Fri 10:00–12:00 and 13:00–16:00, Sun 11:00–16:00

Above: *Berlin's trams operate mainly in the eastern part of the city and its outskirts.*

Berlin Bargain

The Berlin WelcomeCard offers free travel and special reductions in Berlin for two or three days. The WelcomeCard, which allows the holder to take three children up to the age of 14 free, costs 16 euro for two days or 22 euro for three days; it gives price reductions of at least 25% on a wide range of attractions. The SchauLUST Museum Pass gives free admission to more than 70 Berlin museums on three consecutive days.

Tourist Information

The **German National Tourist Office** is represented in the United Kingdom (London), the USA (New York), Canada (Toronto), Japan (Tokyo) and also throughout Europe. The marketing of Berlin is carried out by **Berlin Tourismus Marketing**, ⊠ Am Karlsbad 11, 10785 Berlin, ☎ +49 (30) 26 47 48 0, 📠 +49 (30) 26 47 48 99. There are information offices (Berlin Infostores) at: **Hauptbahnhof (Central Station)**, ⊠ Floor 0, North Entrance, Europa Platz 1 (🕐 08:00–22:00). **Neues Kranzler Eck**, ⊠ Passage, Kurfürstendamm 21 (🕐 Apr–Oct Mon–Sat 10:00–20:00, Sun 10:00–18:00; Nov–Mar daily 10:00–18:00).

Brandenburg Gate, ⊠ South Wing (🕐 Apr–Oct daily 09:30–18:00; Nov–Mar daily 10:00–18:00). **Fernsehturm (TV Tower)**, ⊠ Alexanderplatz (🕐 Apr–Oct daily 09:30–18:00; Nov–Mar daily 10:00–18:00). **Reichstag, Berlin Pavilion**, ⊠ Scheidemannstraße (🕐 Apr–Oct daily 08:00–20:00; Nov–Mar daily 10:00–18:00). **Europa Center**, ⊠ Budapester Straße 45 (🕐 Apr–Oct Mon–Sat 09:00–19:00, Sun 10:00–18:00; Nov–Mar daily 10:00–18:00). There is also a **Berlin-Hotline** for hotel and theatre reservations and tourist information, ☎ +49 (30) 25 00 25, 📠 25 00 24 24.

Embassies and Consulates:

American Embassy, ⊠ Neustädtische Kirchstraße 4–5, 10117 Berlin, ☎ 830 50. **Australian Embassy**, ⊠ Wallstraße 76–79, 10179 Berlin, ☎ 88 00 88 0, 📠 88 00 88 210.

British Embassy, ✉ Wilhelmstraße 70-71, 10117 Berlin, ☎ 204 570, ☏ 2045 7594.
Canadian Embassy, ✉ Leipziger Platz 17, 10117 Berlin, ☎ 203 120, ☏ 2031 2121.
Irish Embassy, ✉ Friedrichstraße 200, 10117 Berlin, ☎ 220 720, ☏ 2207 2299.
South African Embassy, ✉ Tiergartenstraße 18, 10785 Berlin, ☎ 220 730, ☏ 2207 3190.

Entry Requirements

British nationals need a valid passport to enter Germany. Other EU nationals can enter on production of a National Identity Card. Nationals of Australia, Canada, New Zealand and the United States do not need a visa for stays of up to 3 months.

Customs

The duty-free allowance for goods imported into Germany is: one litre of spirits or two litres of fortified wine or two litres of wine, 200 cigarettes (or 50 cigars or 250g tobacco) and 50g perfume. When duty is paid within the EU, the alcohol/tobacco volume is 10 litres of spirits, 20 litres of fortified wine, 90 litres of wine and 110 litres of beer; plus 3200 cigarettes (or 400 cigarillos, 200 cigars or 3kg tobacco).

Health Requirements

No vaccinations are necessary to enter Germany. Free or reduced-cost emergency health treatment is available to British visitors on production of a European Health Insurance Card, which has replaced Form E111 in the UK. All visitors are advised to arrange their own comprehensive travel and medical insurance. Keep receipts and invoices – you will need them when making a claim. (For emergency telephone numbers, *see* Health Services on page 90.)

Getting there

By air: By far the easiest way to get there. Berlin is served by direct flights from 70 countries and there are many more routes involving a change of aircraft elsewhere in Germany. British Airways flies five times daily from London Heathrow to Berlin's Tegel Airport, while low-cost airlines Air Berlin (from London Stansted, Manchester, Glasgow and Belfast), Ryanair (from London Stansted and Nottingham East Midlands) and EasyJet (from London Gatwick, Luton, Bristol, Liverpool, Newcastle, Glasgow and Belfast) also serve Berlin fom the UK. Germany's national airline, Lufthansa, has no direct Berlin flight from the UK, but offers connections through Frankfurt/Main and other German cities. The former East Berlin airport of Schönefeld is being developed to become

Berlin's only international airport; by 2011 it will handle all Berlin flights and Tegel Airport will close. In the meantime, international flights use both Schönefeld, 20km (12 miles) southeast of the city centre, and Tegel, 8km (5 miles) north of the central area. Schönefeld has its own dedicated Airport Express train into the city centre. It operates half-hourly with the same single fare as the U-Bahn and S-Bahn rail networks. Travellers arriving at Tegel have bus links to two U-Bahn (underground) stations: Jakob-Kaiser-Platz (western city) and Kurt-Schuhmacher-Platz (eastern city).

By road: There are excellent motorway connections across Europe on to the Berliner Ring, the Autobahn that surrounds Berlin and provides access to all parts of the city. To drive in Germany, or to hire a car, you need a valid national driving licence. Visitors from Canada, the USA, Australia, New Zealand and South Africa need an international driving licence. Drivers must have green card insurance cover, though this is not compulsory for EU citizens; motoring insurers are increasingly building European cover into their domestic policies, so it pays to shop around. You must also carry the car's registration papers and the red warning triangle compulsory in most European countries. In Germany you drive on the right; drivers must be 18 or older. Seat belts must be worn in the front and back of the car, and children under 12 may not travel in the front seats.

By train: The international train bringing you to Berlin deposits you at the impressive new Berlin Hauptbahnhof, formerly Lehrte Stadtbahnhof, across the River Spree from the Reichstag building and the Spreebogen area of new government buildings. As a key part of city-centre redevelopment, the former S-Bahn station has been turned into a new superstation of glass and steel – it is the largest rail hub in Europe and has taken over the role of the Zoologischer Garten stations. Ongoing investment in Germany's rail network means Berlin can now be reached by the sleek silver-grey ICE (Inter City Express) trains in 1hr 39min from Hanover and in a little over 4hr from Frankfurt am Main.

What to Pack

In **winter**, take your warmest clothing. If it is cold in the west of the city, it will feel bitingly so east of the Tiergarten, with icy winds sweeping in from the Baltic across the city's open squares. Pack your thickest coat, your fur-lined boots and a hat. In **spring** and **autumn**, too, it pays to be sensibly kitted out. Though it is warm when the sun shines, the air cools quickly and evenings can be cold. For **summer**, take light or medium-weight clothing – T-shirt, shorts and swimwear for a lakeside picnic. Though summer in Berlin is rarely excessively hot, sightseeing can be tiring and it is advisable to have a supply of cool cotton clothing. It is worth taking rainwear at any time as Berlin's rainfall occurs year-round. Or pack a fold-up umbrella – it will do the job just as well.

Money Matters

Currency: Germany was one of the first EU countries to embrace the Euro in January 1999.

Credit Cards: Visa, American Express, EuroCard, Diners Club and MasterCard are widely accepted in hotels, shops and restaurants. However, some businesses in the east of the city will accept only cash. There is a 16 per cent VAT levy on goods and services.

Currency exchange: Change money and travellers' cheques at bureaux and banks – look for the Wechsel (exchange) sign. Hotels and some travel agencies will exchange money, but at less favourable rates. Bureaux include **American Express**, ⊠ Bayreuther Straße 37, 10787 Berlin-Schöneberg, ☎ 2147 6292; also ⊠ Friedrichstraße 172, 10117 Berlin-Mitte, ☎ 2017 400; and **Reisebank**, ⊠ Bahnhof Zoo, ☎ 881 7117, and ⊠ Ostbahnhof, ☎ 296 4393.

Tipping: Though restaurants usually include a service charge, it is customary to increase the amount by 5–10 per

Useful Phrases

Do you speak English? • *Sprechen Sie Englisch?*
Goodbye/Bye • *Auf Wiedersehen/Tschüss*
Good day • *Guten Tag*
Good evening • *Guten Abend*
Good morning • *Guten Morgen*
How much is that? • *Wieviel kostet es?*
I (don't) understand • *Ich verstehe (nicht)*
How/When/Where? • *Wie/Wann/Wo?*
Please/Thank you • *Bitte/Danke*
Yes/No • *Ja/Nein*
airport • *der Flughafen*
bill/check • *die Rechnung*
bus • *der Bus*
car • *das Auto*
castle • *das Schloß*
cathedral • *der Dom*
closed • *geschlossen*
departure • *Abfahrt*
entrance • *Eingang*
exit/emergency exit • *Ausgang/Notausgang*
gents • *Herren*
hospital • *Krankenhaus*
identification • *Ausweis*
ladies • *Damen*
menu • *die Speisekarte*
occupied • *besetzt*
passport • *der Pass*
petrol • *das Benzin*
pharmacy • *die Apotheke*
police • *die Polizei*
post office • *das Postamt*
railway station • *der Bahnhof*
street • *die Straße*
ticket • *die Fahrkarte*
timetable • *der Fahrplan*
today • *heute*
tomorrow • *morgen*
train • *der Zug*
tram • *die Straßenbahn*
yesterday • *gestern*

Public Holidays
1 January •
New Year's Day
6 January •
Epiphany
March/April •
Good Friday and
Easter Monday
1 May •
Labour Day
May •
Ascension Day
May/June •
Whit Monday
3 October •
Unity Day
1 November •
All Saints' Day
25 December •
Christmas Day
26 December •
Boxing Day

Left Luggage
There are left luggage facilities at Tegel and Schönefeld airports; also at a number of rail stations, including the Hauptbahnhof and Bahnhof Zoo; there are 24-hour lockers at Friedrichstraße and Alexanderplatz stations.

cent to the nearest round total. For taxi drivers, the recommended tip is the universal 10 per cent, and it is usual to give porters and cloakroom attendants a euro or two. A consideration of between one and three euro, depending on the duration of the tour, is appreciated by tour guides.

City Transport

Berlin's extensive public transport system incorporates the S-Bahn (suburban) and U-Bahn (underground) railways, trams in the eastern part of the city, and buses. It is administered by the BVG (Berliner Verkehrs-Betriebe), which sells single, short-distance, one-day, seven-day and monthly tickets that cover the entire network. Buy your single rail ticket or multijourney ticket from the large yellow or orange ticket machine at the sta-

tion (instructions in English) and validate it in the small red machine on the platform – or at the bus stop. Buy your bus or tram ticket from the driver. For public transport information, ☎ 194 49 for U-Bahn, bus, tram and ferry (24-hour service) and ☎ 2974 3333 for S-Bahn (🕘 Mon–Fri 06:30–22:00, Sat–Sun 07:00–20:00).

Rail: There are 16 **S-Bahn** lines (stations have a white 'S' on a green circle outside). Trains run from around 05:00 until 00:30, with the S7 line (Schönefeld Airport-Westkreuz) operating round the clock at weekends. The nine **U-Bahn** lines operate similar hours, with trains on some lines operating every 15 minutes throughout the night at weekends. The Airport Express train (RE4, RE5) runs between Schönefeld Airport and Zoologischer Garten half-hourly from 05:00 to 23:30 for the cost of a single U-Bahn or S-Bahn ticket.

Buses: Berlin was one of the first cities outside London to operate double-decker buses: seeing the city from the top deck is an obvious attraction. A popular route with tourists is No. 100, which heads east from Zoologischer Garten station, passing the Brandenburg Gate and most of the eastern city sights on its way to Prenzlauer Berg. Night buses replace the S-Bahn and U-Bahn on 54 routes during the time trains are not running: 00:30–04:30. Bus stops are identified by a green 'H' within a yellow circle.

Trams: Berlin's tram network is a legacy from communist times; the 21 lines are mainly in the eastern part of the city and its outskirts. Modern yellow trams have replaced the old ones that trundled through the streets of the former East Berlin, with a few links extended into the west of the city. A good starting point for a tram ride through eastern Berlin is Hackescher Markt, by the S-Bahn station, from where routes radiate towards the distant suburbs.

Car hire: With such a good public transport system, it is seldom necessary to hire a car. If you do need your own transport, hire from the rental desks in Tegel or Schönefeld airport and leave the car at the airport on your way home.

Taxis: There are stands for Berlin's beige-coloured taxis all over town – or you can flag down a cab in the street if its yellow taxi sign is lit up.

Velotaxi rickshaws ply many routes in summer – catch them at designated stops, ☎ 0800 8356 8294.

Bicycles can be hired and, with Berlin's proliferation of cycle lanes, are a good way to get around. Fahrradstation has rental outlets with 2000 bikes for rent across the city, including the main outlet, ✉ Hackesche Höfe, Hof 7, Mitte, ☎ 2838 4848. Others are at ✉ Auguststraße 29A, Mitte, ☎ 2859 9661; ✉ Leipziger Straße 56, Mitte, ☎ 6664 9180; and ✉ Bergmanstraße 9, Kreuzberg, ☎ 215 1566.

Business Hours

Though there are no standard opening hours for shops; usually ⊕ Monday–Friday 09:00–18:30, Saturday 09:00–14:00. They are closed on Saturday afternoon, all day Sunday and public holidays. Recent legislation allows shops to stay open until 20:00 on weekdays and 16:00 on Saturdays. Banking hours are generally ⊕ Monday–Friday 08:30–13:00 and 14:00–16:00 (until 17:30 on Thursday);

the banks do not open on Saturday or Sunday. Airport and railway station *bureaux de change* usually ⏱ 06:00–22:00.

Time Difference

Berlin is on Central European Time, one hour ahead of GMT in winter and two hours ahead of GMT in summer; the 24-hour clock is widely used.

Communications

International telephone calls can be made from public call boxes – dial the following international code first: United Kingdom 0044, Ireland 00353, Australia 0061, Canada and USA 001, New Zealand 0064, South Africa 0027 (don't forget to omit the '0' from the area code). Kiosks take coins and phone cards. Calls from hotels are generally much more expensive – it is far cheaper to dial abroad from a call box and ask the recipient to phone

you back. Tell them to dial 0049 (for Germany), then 30 (for Berlin), followed by the number on the phone in front of you. Useful numbers: Directory enquiries ☎ 11 833; international enquiries ☎ 11 834.

Electricity

The standard continental European 220 volts AC. Two-pin sockets – an adaptor is needed for British and American appliances.

Weights and Measures

Germany uses the metric system. To convert pounds to kilograms, multiply by 0.45 (by 2.21 for the reverse); inches to centimetres, multiply by 2.54 (0.39 for reverse), yards to metres by 0.91 (1.09 for reverse).

Health Services

Medical emergency service, ☎ 31 00 31. Poison emergency service, ☎ 1 92 40. Dental emergency, ☎ 8900 4333.

Drugs emergency service, ☎ 1 92 37. Pharmacy on call (information), ☎ 0 11 89.

Personal Safety

Visitors in any city should guard against petty theft – and Berlin is no exception. Entrust your valuables to the hotel safe rather than leaving them in your room, and beware of pickpockets on crowded public transport and in busy shops. If you have a car, keep valuables out of sight and the vehicle locked and secured. Report any theft to your hotel and the police – if you make an insurance claim you will need a certificate from the police to show they were informed. Credit card insurance is wise: a phone call home in the event of loss can save you having to make international calls to individual companies. Carry photocopies of your passport, air ticket, driving licence and other documents when travelling – they can save no end of hassle later.

Emergencies

Police, ☎ 110.
Fire Brigade, ☎ 112.
Ambulance, ☎ 112.
Gay and Lesbian help is available at ✉ Mommsenstraße 45, Berlin-Charlottenburg, ☎ 2336 9070, ⏰ Mon–Thu 09:00–20:00, Fri 09:00–18:00. Gay and Lesbian hotline: ☎ 19446 216 3336.
Crisis helpline: ☎ 0800 111 0111.
Medical, see Health Services.

Etiquette

It is polite to greet shopkeepers with *Guten Tag* (good day) and *Auf Wiedersehen* (goodbye) on entering and leaving their premises. In crowds, *Entschuldigen Sie bitte* (excuse me please) can help you find a way through. Follow the locals' example and don't jump pedestrian lights – the traffic light sequence may catch you unawares and

you may receive an on-the-spot fine.

Language

Pronunciation of German is not difficult, so do learn a few phrases (see page 87). Though English is widely understood in Berlin – increasingly so in view of the city's recently acquired capital status – you may find it is less so in the eastern part of the city. The locals, as everywhere, will appreciate visitors' efforts to converse in German.

Accommodation

Visitors will find all types of accommodation – from youth hostels and guesthouses to mid-range hotels and the ultimate in five-star luxury. Berlin Tourismus Marketing (🖥 www.berlin-tourist-information.de) gives a complete A to Z of accommodation in the city. Accommodation can be booked in advance on the BTM Hotline, ☎ +49 (30) 25 00 25, 🖷 +49 (30)

25 00 24 24. The service operates Mon–Fri ⏰ 08:00–19:00, Saturday–Sunday and public holidays 09:00–18:00.

Eating Out

Berlin is superbly served by top-quality eating houses – restaurants of every culinary persuasion that range from budget to Michelin-rated. Many open at around 09:30 to serve breakfast – and are still serving it in mid-afternoon. You simply choose English, French, Belgian, German or whatever and tuck in. Hundreds of restaurants serve German fare and hundreds more tempt you with anything from Corsican to Caribbean. They tend to remain open late, often until 01:00 or 02:00. For a quick midday bite, *Imbiss* stands all over the city serve snacks that vary from the ubiquitous burger or filled jacket potato to a plastic bowl piled with Chinese noodles.

INDEX OF SIGHTS

Page numbers given in **bold** type indicate photographs

GENERAL INDEX